I0797768

SHAPING THE WORLD AS A HOME

The Houses & Gardens of Erik Evens

Foreword by

MARC APPLETON

New York · Paris · London · Milan

CONTENTS

FOREWORD

Marc Appleton

I HAVE KNOWN THE ARCHITECT ERIK EVENS as a friend and colleague since he came to work for our firm in 1995. His tenure with us was too short, but he was largely responsible for the design of our Santa Monica office building, which is still our base of operations. Fortuitously he moved on, eventually forming his own successful architectural practice with another close friend, Grant Kirkpatrick. I have been in Erik's fan club ever since, and our paths have happily continued to cross, perhaps most importantly in our shared work for the Southern California chapter of the Institute of Classical Architecture & Art.

Evens has given tirelessly over the years to the ICAA and its mission, teaching drawing and the classical language of architecture to countless students. He calls himself a "Contemporary Classicist" with respect to the classical architectural language and traditions that have informed his work and inspired his philosophical outlook. He is drawn to classical art and architecture because, as he says, "The language of the classical is there to show us the beautiful, and remind us that those things are possible by our hand."

OPPOSITE
A gracious foyer welcomes us to the home while drawing us in. This arched passage from the foyer into the dining room entices us to further explore the secrets of the house.

Although I understand and accept his devotion to the classical tradition, I feel that his work is more broadly based, including regional southern California influences, the actual sites for which he is designing, and a particular responsiveness to his clients' needs and expectations. These latter tendencies are always happily apparent in his work. They may be gently controlled by his respect for classical traditions and proportions, but these other concerns are what bring his projects to life and perhaps account for the "Contemporary" half of the Contemporary Classicist!

This is the first book on his design work, and it is appropriately subtitled: his houses and their gardens are by the same hand, and they complement each other nicely. Typically, most books by residential architects focus on the architecture, not the gardens and the landscapes, which often are designed by independent landscape architects or garden designers, if not by Mother Nature herself. These days we rarely get to appreciate the same designer's hand and eye at work in both arenas.

It wasn't always like this. In the classical tradition, inside and outside were more intimately tied together and interdependent. Architects like Charles A. Platt (1861–1933) were

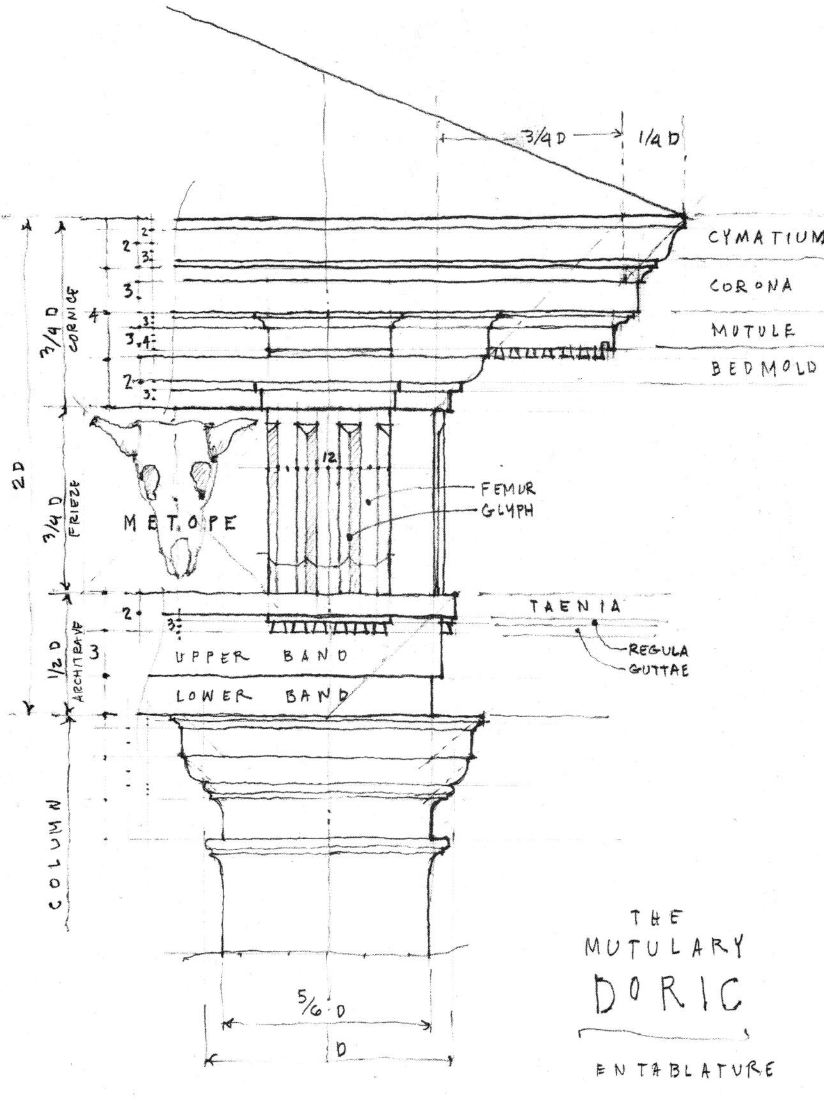

proficient at both. More attention was paid to the design of the garden as an extension of the house, and there was often greater continuity of form and materials connecting the two. With modern and more contemporary architecture, which often seeks a more objective sculptural identity, it seems the two have become less integrated. To be sure, great expanses of glass have allowed the modern house to see more of the outside from inside, but this "fishbowl" effect does not necessarily visually or functionally interconnect the two or focus and frame the connection. It is a pleasure here to see both houses and their gardens depicted together with equal attention and importance.

One of the other appealing things about this book is that it is more modestly written by an architect for homeowners, rather than for other architects or designers. The "values" espoused in the first half of the book are simple, straightforward, unpretentious precepts that Evens indicates have directed his work throughout his career, and they can be easily understood and consumed by the average homeowner: *Place*, *California*, *Proportion*, *Nature*, *Tradition*, *Timelessness*, and *Beauty*. His descriptions of these values are more personal and emotional than academic.

In the value *Place*, when Evens says, "Houses should look like they belong where they are," it seems a simple and direct rule of thumb. More ambitious architects or designers looking for distinguished identity might take issue with this, but generally not those who are in the market for a home, a comfortable, unpretentious, and rewarding place in which to live and raise a family. Evens' different working values are all interrelated, and it's pretty easy to accept their down-to-earth wisdom. When it comes to *Beauty*, for instance, it's accepted as self-evident, an instinctive sense and a part of the admirer's DNA. For Evens, it is "a human necessity."

Evens grew up in Southern California, and his life and experiences in that part of the country clearly color the system of values that guide his professional work. For the most part, his work has focused on the single-family house and property. Varied examples from his overall work, both architecture and landscape, make up the first half of the book. The images loosely illustrate each of the values, featuring details as well as larger views of some of his houses and gardens, and including renovations of older houses that have inspired his values and respect for tradition. True to his own life and by his own admission, there is a predominantly Mediterranean sensibility to the work, which is understandable, given the architectural traditions affecting the history of southern California over the last century.

The second half of the book focuses more particularly on five individual houses and their gardens. They are all architecturally "traditional" but different in style, and range from Spanish Revival to Neo-Colonial to California Bungalow. These stylistic descriptions are fairly loose and do not sufficiently capture the richness of the design effort. It is clear that the architecture for each of these projects is not wedded to a self-consciously traditional mold but is more specifically tailored to each client's expectations and responsive to the particular property location. They are not academic historical exercises but speak to more intimate family lifestyles and occupancy.

In each of the five projects there are eclectic elements here and there that show his clients' involvement, and Evens seems comfortable in gracefully accommodating them. These are, after all, family homes where the presence of children is apparent. They have been tidied up, as is typical for photo shoots, but one has the sense that once the photographer has left, family life and a less staged and more messy occupancy will quickly return. These places look livable, something often missing in houses where the architect's or designer's personal stamp is too self-conscious or dominant.

Concurrent with this, one also senses that sometimes there were client-driven inclinations for a more contemporary, light-filled interior design within the initial traditional impulses driving the architecture. This is often a common challenge for traditionally inclined residential architects, especially those of us inspired by regional, traditional, or vernacular precedents and their proportions: the contemporary elements can clash or seem out of scale, seeking to raise ceilings or open up spaces that traditionally want to be more discreetly designed and detailed. A large expanse of undivided glass, for example—the

floor-to-ceiling "picture window"—can awkwardly explode a space that traditionally was defined by the smaller-scale divided-glass windows that were part of an earlier vocabulary. Here again Evens seems up to the task of successfully negotiating these compromises.

In the Parra Grande project these challenges are not only met but, in the process, result in an especially elegant dialogue between house and garden. There is a strong relationship between inside and outside spaces that is implicit not only in the repetition of the architectural forms used for both but also in the materials, particularly the predominant use of local sandstone for walls and columns.

The design encourages these connections by creating outdoor dining and sitting areas, terraced gardens, and a vine-covered pergola, all sharing the warm sandstone. The used-brick, flagstone, gravel, and decomposed granite patios and pathways flow together seamlessly and are surrounded with lavender, olives, and other plantings that create a relaxed, informal Mediterranean garden environment. At its edges this cultivated landscape visually transitions into the surrounding native background habitat of California live oak, pine, and eucalyptus. House and garden seem one, indoors and outdoors harmoniously ambiguous.

This project also includes a delightful destination pool and pool house. The pool house architecture is a traditional cross-gabled plan suggesting Palladian inspiration. It is otherwise more "California Ranch" contemporary and light-filled, with large sliding doors and a glass pediment brightening a comfortably furnished contemporary sitting area overlooking the pool.

The unique design of the pool also reinforces the concept of an ambiguous indoor-outdoor relationship, this time between the central swimming section, which at its barely underwater edge intermixes with and is surrounded by a more natural pondlike environment that includes water lilies and other aquatic plants. One is, in effect, swimming in a pond, but without the muddy water or nuisance of unwanted critters and insects. I would hazard a guess, however, that occasional frogs or migrating waterfowl might find it equally attractive, further enhancing the ambiguity.

Parra Grande seems an elegant example of the richness that can evolve from the architect's design integration of house and garden as well as a sophisticated and compatible marriage of the traditional and contemporary, formal and informal. Here Evens' values of *Place*, *California*, *Proportion*, *Nature*, *Tradition*, *Timelessness*, and *Beauty* all seem harmoniously present in one project. With this book, we are now the beneficiaries along with his clients.

OPPOSITE From my sketchbook, this drawing of the Mutulary Doric entablature was constructed during an ICAA class.

ABOVE Early in the process, a drawing is an opportunity to tease out the character of the architecture; the design is developed while creating drawings such as this.

INTRODUCTION

Erik Evens

I wasn't born an architect. I wasn't the child who spent countless hours building houses out of Lincoln Logs, or cities out of Legos. My early teachers didn't summon my parents to school for meetings where they prophesized an architectural career. Though eventually that did come to pass, those early years were really about my absorption in two realms: craft and art. Years later, their synthesis became the work I've dedicated myself to for four decades: architecture.

Looking back, it makes so much sense. Craft is concerned with the pragmatics of making things, and art is concerned with the aesthetics of beautiful things. It's math and beauty, the mechanical and the sublime, and growing up, I was fortunate to be exposed to both.

When it came to working with his hands, my father was masterful. Many of my best memories lead back to the same place: the home shop and working side by side with my dad. Some days we'd make furniture, other days we'd fix things; something was always going on, and often that included sailboats. With our box of tools in hand, we would go down to the marina and do maintenance work on our sailboat, a lovely little Scandinavian boat built out of mahogany. It's often said that time messing around with boats is time well spent. I loved it, and really, what was *not* to love? Not only did I get to spend time on the boat, but I also got to touch it, to run my hands over it, and be engaged with all aspects of its care and maintenance. My father taught me so many technical things; he also taught me the love of doing those things.

OPPOSITE
White hand-troweled plaster, warm terra-cotta paving, and lushly colored geometric tile—these classic elements of the Mediterranean vernacular are all designed to draw us in.

Then there was the other side of me, the side that was always drawing, sketching, or painting. The ability to visualize in three dimensions came naturally to me, with things flowing easily from my head to my hand, and into a sketchpad. Whatever I was passionate about, I depicted there. From dinosaurs, I progressed to cars, and then to boats, and just about any other type of vehicle. What was I *not* drawing? Houses. At least not yet. My appreciation for architecture came later, and not surprisingly, I entered it through art.

My first year at UCLA as an art major saw me working my way through a course load of pre-reqs, from basics of design, to critical inquiry, to design philosophy, which came with an interesting Bauhaus spin. Finally, I took an elective. It was called something like

"Modern Architecture in the 20th Century," and it would change the trajectory of my life. A survey class, it was taught by Thomas Hines. In addition to being a Neutra scholar and a great author, Professor Hines was also a wonderful teacher.

Being exposed to the innovative architects in California, including Frank Lloyd Wright, Richard Neutra, and especially Rudolph Schindler, caused a light to go on for me. In their work, I saw the intersection of the pragmatic and the aesthetic, of craft and art. Everything came together for me in that class, and I knew what I wanted to do. I immediately applied to architecture schools, was accepted, left UCLA, and headed north, to the central coast of California, and CalPoly San Luis Obispo.

I never looked back, never had a second thought. Architecture appealed to me in many ways, and not just the big two of craft and art. Architecture also offered me a very human connection. I am blessed to be able to work closely with people.

For me, an ongoing attraction of architecture is that we do it for others. Through our work, architects are able to touch people, and make their world a better place. Even in the commercial and institutional projects I've done, at its core, the work was conceived for people. That focus is especially acute in my residential practice, and it is what makes me particularly happy. Learning about my clients, responding to them through my understanding of their lives, their needs and wants, fulfills me. When I am able to work with my clients in this very direct way, I have a kind of satisfaction I didn't have as a fine artist. For as fulfilling as that was, it didn't put me on the path of others, and over the years I've found that I love being on that path.

The experience of telling other people's stories through their homes is a continuation of another lifelong love. As a young man, devouring literature, poetry, and the great novels, I not only loved the analysis of books, but I also loved creating elaborate visual images in my mind. I saw what I was reading as a movie unspooling in my head, a "mind movie" of literature. In a way, my process for creating architecture is like that, too; it's crafting a narrative and bringing it to life. When I'm thinking about the architecture we're doing for a client, I'm creating a mind movie, this time of their home and how their life will unfold within it.

Still, architecture is more than that. It has to be. Why else would I remain committed to it, and compelled by it, after so many years of practice? I believe the answer lies in the insights into human nature that continue to engage me. There are many great mysteries in the world. Among the most beguiling of them is beauty. Within all of us is a need to see and to be in touch with beauty. For me, the search has been to try to begin to understand it. Sometimes that path has been dimly lit, and it's been hard for me to see clearly and difficult to define. But despite the challenges, I know that the journey is worthy of the effort. When I stop and ask myself why, I inevitably return to the same answer: because my innate need for the beautiful nurtures my soul.

Beauty is a human necessity for me, and it's a gift. Opening that gift, beauty brings an affirmation of my life, my existence, and my life's work as an architect. The philosopher Roger Scruton says it in a way that has inspired me for many years: "Through the pursuit of beauty we shape the world as a home."

Contemplating a beautiful work of art, whether it's a painting, a sculpture, or any other kind of individual expression of creativity, helps us to endure the chaos of life, and it also can bring us joy and solace. Yes, life can be challenging, but seeing and creating beauty is my antidote for that, reminding me of the things that really matter.

That is why I'm drawn to classical art and architecture. The language of the classical is there to show us the beautiful, and remind us that those things are possible by our hand. While the classical language is my preferred mode, and I see it as a particularly steadfast way to create beauty, I know it's not the only way. Modernist architecture can do that as well.

But no matter the aesthetic language we choose, the key is that it must address and reflect our nature as humans. We are hardwired to perceive certain proportions, and certain geometries, as beautiful. It's right there in front of us when we look at the deep complexity of nature. There, we see an intimate relationship between the scale of the large and the scale of the small, the branches of a tree to its leaves, the rose to its individual petals, the mountain to its range. And when we step back and take in those multiple scales, our "wiring" allows us to see them as beautiful. Classical architecture has evolved over centuries to become finely tuned to us as human beings. It seeks to tap into this basic form of beauty, and when it succeeds, it allows us to acknowledge and connect to our human nature.

As a contemporary classicist, my highest aspiration is to create homes for people that remind them of the beautiful. If I can provide this connection, if my clients can live surrounded by beauty, and thrive in it, then perhaps in my own way I am "shaping the world as a home" for them. Ultimately, this is the essence of what I want to achieve through my work: to design environments for people that give them gracious shelter, offer them comfort, and open a door to joy for them. The best way I know how to do that is by infusing their houses with beauty.

OPPOSITE Dining in the out-of-doors is a welcome opportunity to appreciate the beauty surrounding us.

VALUES

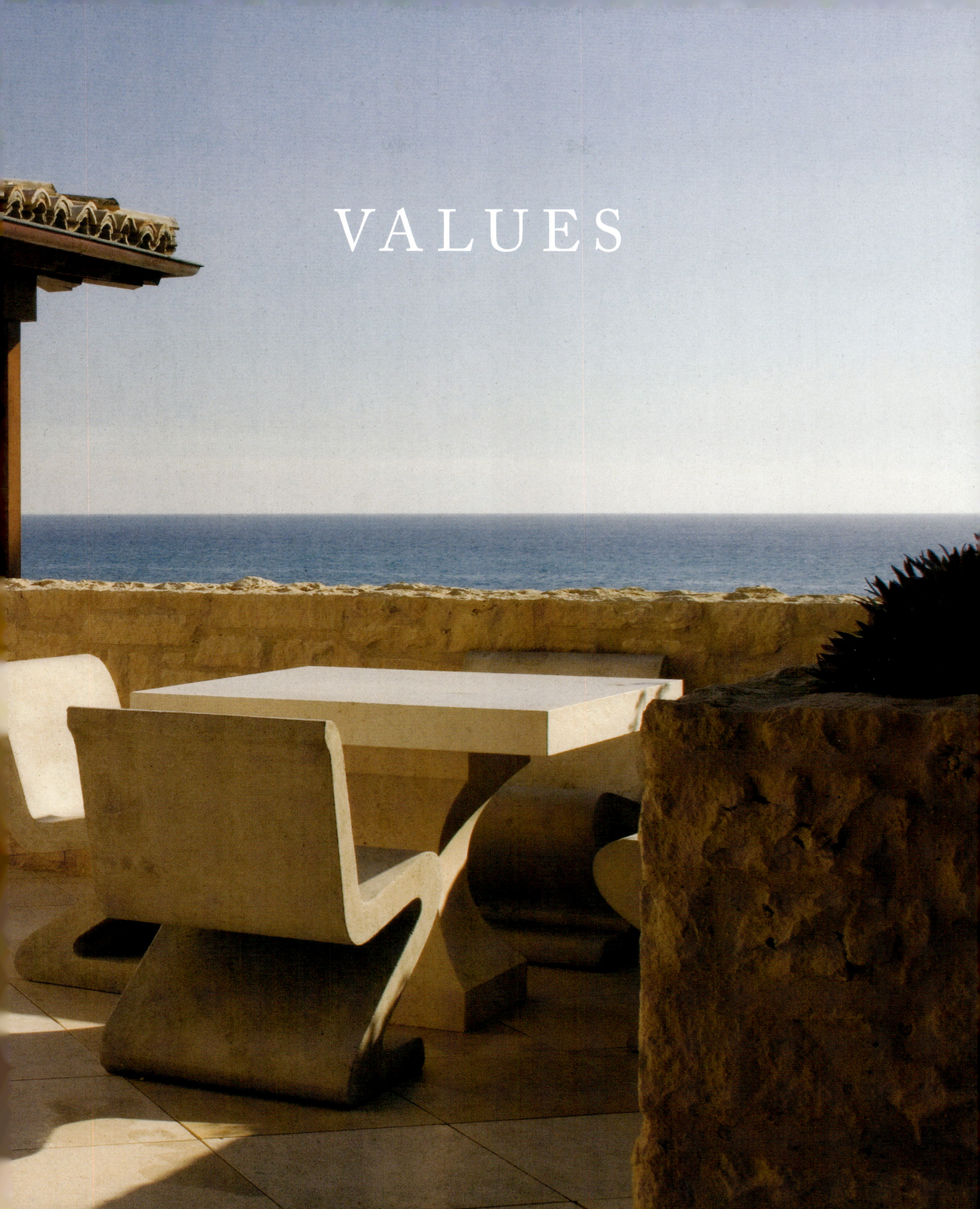

PLACE

"If you don't know where you are, you don't know who you are."
—WENDELL BERRY

Houses should look like they belong where they are. This seemingly simple sentence is foundational to how I approach my work. To me, creating a sense of belonging for the house is a way of creating a similar sense of belonging for the people living in it. It's almost a form of reassurance: "If the building belongs here then maybe I do, too." In the building's rightness of place, we derive great comfort; in architecture's ability to tie us to our locale, we find security, support, and connection. If there is a better way to explain "belonging," I'm not sure I've found it.

I don't think you need to be an architect to grasp this idea. Haven't we all walked into a building that just felt so right, so perfect in its particular place? It's happened to me on many occasions, often with Southern California architecture. Each time I'm in Santa Barbara or Montecito and take in one of the great Mediterranean-style houses of George Washington Smith, I can feel my body respond to what I'm seeing: I breathe more slowly, I feel at ease. The Spanish Colonial Revival houses and civic buildings he designed are quite at home in California. By tapping into long-standing building traditions, he created a sense of belonging to a place. Today, when I design a Mediterranean house for Southern California, I am deliberately seeking to reinforce the personality of that place by designing within the framework of this great tradition, a tradition so well established that, by tapping into its wellspring, we can readily create buildings that respond to their locale.

I feel a similar sense of rightness in the Venetian countryside, when I consider the villas of Andrea Palladio. There is a kind of perfection about them; they look and feel as though they belong there, and there alone. The villas have a singular relationship with the

RIGHT & FOLLOWING The Mediterranean character of the house melds easily with its Southern California locale. The thoughtfully crafted architecture evokes the romance of life in old California.

LEFT
Teak shutters, white painted woodwork, and characteristic broad eaves help this Caribbean Colonial house feel at home next to the blue Pacific.

OPPOSITE
In the desert environment, there's great appreciation for the Spanish Mediterranean's deep overhangs and their ability to perform their primary function: providing shade.

RIGHT
An outdoor courtyard offers shelter from the desert's hot, dry winds and searing sun.

surrounding landscape, and the architecture's association with the rich cultural history of the Veneto reinforces the feeling that it simply could not be any other way.

Approaching the design of a building by capturing its sense of place can make for an enormously integrated environment. This is why Bath, England, is one of my favorite cities. It presents itself with great harmony and consistency, and I find such beauty in that. A select group of Georgian architects—notably John Wood the Elder, his son John Wood the Younger, and Robert Adam—were responsible for designing much of the core of the city. They used the same creamy Bath limestone for all the Palladian-inspired neoclassical architecture there. Walking from one street to the next, there's a striking consistency that elicits one of the strongest senses of place I have experienced in any city. I could be teleported onto one of Bath's streets and within a moment I'd know where I was. It's not that the buildings are all the same; within the narrow range of architectural style, you find great variation. The greatest places are the ones that have this quality, such as the French Quarter in New Orleans. Its buildings are generally straightforward and recognizable: two or three stories, iron railings, second-floor balconies. But within the range of that stylistic framework lies wide variation, and what emerges from it is the personality of the city.

As a born and raised Angeleno, I yearn for that type of deep expression of a city's persona. Often, my city doesn't fulfill my yearning. It doesn't make me love Los Angeles less so much as cause me to consider all the ways it could be better. Driving from one building site to another—from my office to my home, and all routes in between—allows me to imagine an alternative history. "What ifs" are raised, and a fantasy city soon emerges. Rather than vast stretches of over-developed buildings sitting in under-cared–for surroundings, what if there were buildings designed in a recognizable tradition and a community that truly loved and cherished them? What if that pride allowed the buildings to stand for years, decades, and perhaps centuries, thereby establishing a true sense of place? And there, among the surrounding slopes, green coastal hillsides, and blue Pacific, we'd see our architectural lineage, stretching back across time and continents. There is no doubt that thoughts like this help pass the time on the road, and in school drop-off and pick-up lines. But there's more to them; they serve as daily reminders of all that could be. They shape my thoughts about what I am trying to achieve in my work, and thus hone my point of view, and my practice.

My goal is to create buildings with a strong sense of place that contribute to a quality of timelessness, buildings that evoke the feeling that not only do they belong where they stand but that they've always been there. On a human level, that kind of inevitability of a place comes with a strong emotional component. It connects us to something greater than our tiny spot in this little moment. A building that feels right in its locale allows us to connect to a tradition that takes us from the ancestors who came before us to the descendants who will live there when we're gone.

OPPOSITE Beautiful when new, Spanish Colonial Revival architecture grows into its mature beauty under the patina of age.

CALIFORNIA

"In your arms, by the ocean. Surrounded by the starry, dreamy sky.
Wrapped-up with the warmth of a bonfire.
Lit-up by our love for the universe—California."
—FARAH AYAAD

My earliest memories of living in California are of a tiny house tucked right up against the San Gabriel Mountains in La Crescenta, whose northern border is the Angeles National Forest. I remember the wildfires coming down the mountain and being scared, and seeing bobcats walking along the streets who, for some reason, were not scared. We lived there until I was seven, when we moved to the San Fernando Valley, and into a great 1940s California Ranch house.

To anyone fortunate enough to have their life unfold in a California Ranch house, the term probably means something quite specific. To me, one of the fortunate, it means a house that supports an outdoor-living lifestyle—all year round. For my family, it meant big sliding doors that opened onto our large, covered veranda. Out there, even in the summer's full heat, we cooked, ate, and played. Our house had a cedar shake roof, cedar lap siding, and big diamond-paned windows. My job was to repair and paint the windows, an assignment that taught me the craft of caring for wood window frames and mullions—a job that never seemed to end.

The kind of outdoor living I grew up with is always present in my work, always emphasizing my belief that life in the out-of-doors is to be cherished. Today, with inescapable air conditioning, home theaters, and extraordinarily large TV screens for viewing and gaming, a strong gravitational pull tugs us towards an indoor orbit, away from fully appreciating what California so generously provides in abundance: a benign climate and great beauty. Architecture has the ability to change that. It can redirect our attention, making it impossible for us to ignore the nature that awaits just outside our doors and

RIGHT A synthesis of architecture and landscape, the pergola is a lovely structure unto itself; yet, enveloped in greenery and vines, it's also a living expression of our relationship with the natural world.

windows. My work often finds me configuring, or reconfiguring, a house so that its outdoor spaces are not simply passed through on the way to somewhere else, but are actually there to draw us in, encourage us to relax and linger, gather and dine, and ultimately, to play a central role in our daily lives.

Being a contemporary classical architect in California has always felt perfectly natural to me. The climate, especially in the southern part of the state, is Mediterranean, and remarkably similar to that of southern Italy, France, Spain, and northern Africa, where the roots of classicism first took hold. I suspect the first Spanish missionaries who settled here found it easy to transplant that familiar style; it's a great fit in a climate that reminded them of their home. The kind of architecture that works well in California also has tremendous allure to people in other parts of the US and the world. Clients come to us from all over, saying, "we want a California house," because they find the architecture and the lifestyle it supports so appealing.

Beyond the climate, there are other things about my home state that serve as daily inspiration. The diverse characteristics of its regions and cities are of constant interest: San Diego is different from Los Angeles, which is vastly different from the Central Coast, which is distinct from the Central Valley, San Francisco, and the desert. All are varied, unique places, all the way up to the mountains, from the Sierra Nevada to the Cascades. Yet, there are throughlines—namely, regional architecture that connects people to nature, and the mindset.

California, for me and many before me, has the air of a place where anything is possible. It's a place where people have always gone to explore new things, to live unencumbered by the strain of history. I feel its impact in architecture, in an approach that isn't quite so doctrinaire, where one might choose not to follow all the rules. The result is architecture that's a little less buttoned-up, a bit more eclectic, and more open to exploring new configurations. I'm interested in taking the language of a particular style and using it to say something different. While I see my work as part of the classical tradition, I also see it as not always fitting comfortably in that mold, and being open and welcoming of the idiosyncratic.

A born and bred Californian, I feel the pull of the unexpected. Does living in earthquake country have anything to do with this? Perhaps. But it definitely shows up in my work in design elements that aren't strictly expected or even necessary, that are there simply because they add something emotionally. They're fanciful. They give people reasons to love the architecture beyond its pragmatism. They stir the soul.

This is the ongoing fascination and endless inspiration that California gives me. It has the capacity to stir my soul, over and over.

PREVIOUS & LEFT Architecture that opens into the landscape is quintessentially Mediterranean. This house has two options to extend out: the main loggia off the living room and a destination entertainment loggia off the kitchen. Permanently furnished, they take full advantage of year-round outdoor living.

LEFT &
OPPOSITE
Refining the Mediterranean style for its seaside locale meant paring back the language of the architecture. And rather than highly embellished details for moldings and decoration, we opted for simplicity to offer no competition with the view, and an elemental backdrop for life outdoors.

Throughout the years I've traveled and have often imagined living in other places: Florence, Paris, Lisbon . . . I can see myself living in any one of those cities. Then I come home and fall in love with California again and realize how lucky I am to live here. So lucky to walk outside my door and feel the sunshine on my back and smell the ocean air. Lucky to go sailing on almost any day of the year, and for a part of the year, to grab my skis and head to the mountains. I want my work to give other people the chance to live like this, to make it easy for them to thoughtfully connect to nature, and to fall in love with the home that enables them to do that.

RIGHT The California live oaks were here long before our architecture, so we deferred to them, designing places under, around, and near their sheltering branches to enjoy life unfolding in beauty.

FOLLOWING There's an almost magical feeling to the way this natural pool blurs the border between the man-made and nature's realm.

PROPORTION

"A great building, in my opinion, must begin with the unmeasurable, must go through measurable means when it is being designed, and in the end must be unmeasurable."
—LOUIS KAHN

Proportion is a foundational principle in classical architecture. It's often approached in a rigorous, mathematical way, which may be the reason some critics, some modernists, and even some philosophers reject it. They see its mathematical underpinning as a form of mental gymnastics, a subject divorced from the details of human life. I understand that it may seem abstract, and at times abstruse, yet in the realm of people living in the homes I design, it's anything but that. There, proportion is not only clear and relatable, it also affects the way they experience their house on a daily basis.

The practical essence of proportion might be described this way: Everything in a building should be properly related to everything else in the building. The very small bits should relate to very large bits in a sensible way. Nature operates with the same strategy. Smaller components always seem to relate to and reiterate the whole: the veins in the leaves of the tree relate to and remind us of the form of the tree's branches . . . the branches to the trunk, the trunk to the roots. It's hard not to find inspiration in nature, and my work is always elevated when I take its lessons to heart.

In any piece of architecture, the individual parts should relate to one another as if they are members of a family talking to each other. This "family of things" can be viewed as a collection of discrete parts that have individual character. Yet, at the same time, they work together to create a holistic form, singular unto itself. When this happens, the building becomes a happy, functional family made of members, who are relating to each other harmoniously. This is important to any building, but in a house it's absolutely essential. Our home is our place in the world; in it, each part needs to be scaled

RIGHT The rhythm and pattern in the Moroccan tile speak to us at the fine scale, which we reiterated in the large scale of the architecture.

LEFT & OPPOSITE
Geometry is at play in the primary bathroom through the starburst motif. Established in the detailing of the wainscoting's small tile, it relates to the larger detailing of the bathtub's wood canopy, the light fixture, and then up to the ceiling, where the starburst appears in sculptured plaster.

thoughtfully, not only to all the other parts, but most importantly to people, as we too are members of the "family of things."

Designing a doorway, I'll carefully consider proportion to ensure its main dimensions, height and width, will be in the right ratio, that allowing people to feel comfortable. Chances are good I'll look to the 2:1 Roman classical ratio, a proportion that's been called into service for thousands of years because it is just so pleasing to the eye. Within that range we feel at ease, and we are drawn to it. Proportional ratios let me use the architecture to communicate: "This is your sanctuary. Relax. You belong here."

Developing ceiling heights, I'll call on proportion once again. To facilitate a person's enjoyment in a room of their house, I'll be searching for the perfect ratio of the area of the room to the height of its ceiling. My goal? To create a space that relates to the human form in a way that enhances one's feelings of comfort and safety. Walk into a great cathedral with its vast soaring spaces and notice how all of its geometry is leading your eye upwards. The proportional ratio I worked so hard to make just right in my client's house is decidedly *not* the same ratio at work in the sanctuary of a great church. In that context, the architecture is saying, "Remember your place in the world. Remember you are small. Be awed by this; be humble."

Architects have many tools of our trade. Even in our digital design world, there are some old school tools I still use: sketch paper, compass, triangle, and pencil—I have them all on my desk—but there is none I love using more than my proportional divider. This tool allows me to make sure I'm designing with proportions that create a particular sense of contentment. When designing a doorway, I might set it to a 2:1 ratio, do a quick check, and adjust as necessary. Even early in my design process, when I'm just sketching and laying things out, it helps me see if I'm within a happy range. Proportion doesn't have to be absolutely exact; just entering its forgiving sweet spot causes our perception to respond favorably. My fascination with this kind of geometric rigor doesn't end with doorways and ceilings. It extends to siting the building on the property in relation to the street, or to the shape of swimming pools and their relation to the landscape. That flows from my belief that humans are hardwired to appreciate certain proportions.

There are always choices for us to make in terms of how we see the world. Will it be as a collection of discrete pieces that all relate to each other in a rational and scientific way? Or will we see the world as a whole form, and react to it emotionally? There are days I'll walk into a building, take measurements, analyze the bits, and experience the intellectual satisfaction that brings. But it's just as true that there are days I'll walk into a magnificent concert hall and simply let its beauty wash over me. I don't need to know it has a 2:1 doorway ratio to know that I feel great walking through it. Both are necessary for a complete understanding, and I am grateful that I can have both. Science and art, intellect and emotion are overlapping lenses through which I can experience the world, and it's a blessing to live with both of them. It's also a gift to know that within each of those realms I can dive in deeply, and come away feeling equally nourished. The language of classical architecture makes sure of it.

PREVIOUS LEFT Wall tile by Moroccan craftspeople, using ages-old methods of tilework, presents an example of using traditional architecture to create interest at the fine scale.

PREVIOUS RIGHT The gallery hallway forms the main connective spine of the house. Its groined vaulting is geometrically rigorous, resulting in a hypnotic rhythm of shade and light on the ceiling.

OPPOSITE A close-up of the entablature; its fine-scale molding details draw us in.

LEFT
Our design study for the details of the Ionic capital and entablature of a Los Angeles home.

OPPOSITE
Bertram Goodhue's ceiling at Mi Sueño, which we brought back to life. A restoration painter, channeling Michelangelo, lay on his back on scaffolding for weeks to reveal its former glory.

OPPOSITE & RIGHT
All the elements relate to one another, becoming a cohesive whole, like the words of a poem acting together to express a unified idea.

NATURE

"Whoever you are, no matter how lonely,
the world offers itself to your imagination,
calls to you like the wild geese, harsh and exciting—
over and over announcing your place
in the family of things."
—MARY OLIVER

I grew up in a family that always seemed to be out in nature. My father was an outdoorsman: a sailor, a skier, a scuba diver, an ethical hunter who ate what he took down. To this day, I'm grateful to him for sharing all of this with me, the things that stuck, and the things that didn't. My mother played a large part in all of our outdoor adventures. Having grown up in what I think of as "old California," amid acres and acres of avocado orchards in La Cañada, her appreciation of nature seemed to be rooted in those trees. When our family moved to the San Fernando Valley in the early 1960s, its whole northern reaches were filled with orchards of citrus trees—grapefruit, orange, and lemon. On a typical summer day, I'd take off on my bike and ride and ride, nabbing a few oranges to refresh myself during the summer heat. And when I think of the many things I love about architecture, one is its ability to provide its own kind of connection to the natural world.

Architecture can, and I believe should, offer opportunities for human beings to relate to nature. At its best, traditional architecture does exactly that. As an architect, I see it as my responsibility to provide these opportunities, whether through carefully composed vistas, or a perfectly placed window with a view of a canyon below. I seek to continue the traditions put forth by architects in the ancient world, who saw their work in part as a way to remind us of our proper place in the universe. As humans, we occupy this place for now; nature reminds us that there is more beyond.

RIGHT Seamlessly, and seemingly effortlessly, architecture and nature become intertwined, with landscaped outdoor destination areas providing places for retreat and contemplation.

Going through life, we are both a part of nature and apart from nature; my work is about providing ways to straddle the two. Loggias, verandas, and courtyards are responses to our innate desire to connect with nature while still remaining a part of the human-made world, connected to our history, culture, and other people. These spaces are our transition from inside to outside. Open to the air, to the breezes that bring the smell of flowers, and to the sounds of birds, crickets, and leaves rustling in the wind, they let us engage in a constant dialogue with nature, yet not be fully in nature. We are still within the structure of the building, still buffered against the harsher aspects of nature. These spaces are saying, "here there's safety and comfort." We are apart from hostile forces. At the same time, the architecture says, "here is a threshold, a path to the natural world."

Entering the house, it is important to maintain this connection to nature. A bedroom needs to feel enclosed and safe, but its windows should offer vistas to remind us of where we are on the planet. A library needs to have smaller windows in one part of a room to mitigate the intrusion of sunlight for book preservation, but the other side of the room might have a large wall of windows to allow in more natural light for reading, or gazing outdoors and contemplating our place in the world. A courtyard provides another way to be in nature, albeit a controlled experience. The sky is above us, but here below we are protected. It's an architectural feature explored and perfected in ancient Greece and Rome, as well as in the Americas with the Alta California Missions.

The language of traditional architecture also accesses nature through decoration, embedding elements within its design that remind us of nature. In floral or vegetal embellishment of moldings, our architecture references nature explicitly. There's a more implicit way to do it as well, and that is by structuring the architecture to have engaging detail at multiple scales.

Imagine you are on a hike in the wilderness, and you reach a clearing, where an old oak tree is visible on a distant hilltop. It's a picturesque silhouette against the sky. Closer, you see its structure more clearly, the branching of its trunk like outward-stretching limbs; you notice a rhythm to its branching. Closer still, you see much more detail, its craggy bark full of crevices and textures that are rough to the touch. Up close, you examine one of its leaves and note its delicacy. You become aware that its structure reiterates the branching scheme you saw at the larger scale. The natural world, abounding in intriguing form, geometry, and texture, has just activated your senses by employing those elements in a variety of scales.

When I encounter traditional architecture, my experience is remarkably similar. I look at a building in the distance and see its overall form, an engaging silhouette against the sky. As I approach, I start to see the smaller-scale elements of the architecture, its columns, beam work, and eaves. Closer still, the moldings of the architecture engage me, with the delicate play of shade and shadow upon their surfaces. As close as possible now, I see that the moldings themselves are embellished with an egg-and-dart motif, or perhaps with a leaf-and-dart, or a classic Greek key. The world of this building has just activated my senses by using form, geometry, and captivating details at a variety of scales.

Traditional architecture, by intentionally emulating nature, reminds us of the natural world, and we can partake of its virtues in the homes we make for ourselves. We may feel calm, comforted, and present. We might feel encouraged, moved, or motivated. Sitting down at my drafting table, I'm aware that designing a house in nature is creating something that's not part of nature, yet the natural world is still there. It's always there. I want to preserve a connection to it, and at the same time, I want our homes to say something thoughtful about what that connection should be. This connection can be a source of inspiration throughout the day, but it's always a reminder of where we've come from.

PREVIOUS Architecture that meanders and opens up to engage with the landscape on the main level offers a variety of places to find refuge.

OPPOSITE A portal to the natural world crafted through architecture.

FOLLOWING Encounters with nature become moments of soul-soothing replenishment.

OPPOSITE
& RIGHT
Spaces where we can reside in the middle ground between architecture and the natural world are highly valued by our clients.

LEFT
With the beach just a few feet away and the surf line a little farther, the protected veranda makes living adjacent to nature easy. Shuttered doors cut the wind, while pocketing steel doors extend the living room into the outdoor-indoor space.

TRADITION

"History is a gift, not an imposition."
—WITOLD RYBCZYNSKI

When I was a young boy, my parents had a sailboat. It was a small craft, 28 feet long, lovingly built of mahogany in Sweden. Many glorious, sunlit days were spent sitting on the aft deck of that humble Nordic boat as we sailed to the Channel Islands for weekends, lying at anchor in one of the cozy coves there. The majestic grace and elegant profile of a classic sailing craft has always filled me with wonder. The magnificent shape of a sailboat hull has always seemed to me to be the perfect synthesis of form and function.

Thinking about my career as an architect, it is clear to me that my aesthetics have been shaped by my time spent in and around sailboats. The parallels between the design of great sailboats and the design of great buildings are undeniable. Specific hull shapes allow the water to slip over them more smoothly than others, and particular hull configurations keep the choppy seas from crashing over the bow. Certain sail designs capture the wind more efficiently and allow the boat to move through the water more quickly. All of these pragmatic constraints, and all of the science and engineering behind them, are carefully considered in the design of sailboats. But none of this is of any consequence if it results in boats that are not beautiful to the eye. And so it is with architecture. We can create technological marvels and solve practical problems, such as resisting gravity, to produce buildings that address functional needs. All are essential concerns for me as a designer, but if I do not also create beauty, do not design buildings which stir our souls, excite our senses, and provide an appropriate backdrop, a proper tableau for human endeavor, then I believe I have fallen short.

Traditions in the design of buildings, like those in the design of sailboats, become finely tuned to our human nature over time; to

RIGHT & FOLLOWING Amid plantings of olive trees and bougainvillea, the rough and textured materials speak their own rustic California dialect of the archetypal Mediterranean language.

ICON
ICONS FROM SINAI
THE GLORIOUS CONSTELLATIONS

me, that's what makes them invaluable. Architecture and the arts have evolved alongside human civilization. There's ongoing feedback between public taste and human aspiration, and the architect must respond to all. Over time, that feedback results in a finely tuned language of architecture embedded in that tradition. In my work, I tap into the wisdom of architectural languages aligned with those traditions.

I consider myself a contemporary classicist. While every project does not specifically employ the language of classicism, I always employ it philosophically. It's my worldview, my way to make art; it's my way to reflect the collected wisdom of our culture, and to endeavor to maintain the continuity from generation to generation.

There's a reason people respond to traditional architecture; it gives us something we need as human beings: it connects us with our past, with those who came before us, and their accomplishments. It's a gift to us from preceding generations, and it's one that I gratefully accept and endeavor to expand upon. It's why I believe there's value in aligning my design with a great tradition. And it's why I work with clients to identify a specific tradition and then use it as a starting point, explicitly or implicitly.

Tradition, and all it encompasses, is so much deeper than what is sometimes written off as a "pastiche," or "nostalgia." It speaks to the persistence of human nature, and raises questions I love to consider: Is it reasonable to think that those things that appealed to our ancestors might appeal to us now? Are we so different from our ancestors? I hope not; I'm comforted by the idea that we're the same in so many ways to a Roman citizen—in our wonder about the natural world; in our need for safety, comfort, shelter, and warmth, the things that signify home; in our desire for love, both platonic and romantic. We're not so different, and so it follows that the same aesthetics would appeal to us in a similar way today as they did back then.

When someone sees a home I've done, and says, "Hey, that's different, I like that," I'm incredibly happy. I'm just as happy as when someone sees something and says, "That's really great, it reminds me of something I saw back when I was in Provence." It means I've successfully tapped into an idea or memory, maybe connected a dot or two, and have touched someone. And so, perhaps what I've done will take hold and go forward. That is what tradition does, when it succeeds, it latches on, because it represents the collective mind, the accumulated wisdom of humanity. Deciding to embrace that, and take advantage of it means using traditional architecture to remind us of our proper place in the cosmos. Palladio's Villa La Rotonda, outside Vicenza, sitting amid olive trees on a hilltop with the vast sky above, is whispering to us, "here is our place, this wondrous middle ground between earth and heaven."

It's not unlike the feelings I had when I was on the water for those long days and nights of summer sailing with my family. For hours on end, I'd lay on the deck staring up at the vast and unfathomable sky, sailing across the vast and unfathomable ocean. And as the water rushed sonorously off the bow of this lovely, lonely little boat, I was aware that it contained all the people I loved and it was keeping all of us safe, while occupying that glorious middle ground. And somehow, despite being on the water, that thought grounded me.

OPPOSITE White plaster walls and elements of hand-hewn wood, reminiscent of the Spanish missions, provide the ideal setting for our client's collection of religious artworks.

LEFT
Tying yesterday to today through traditional architectural detailing painted in modern blue lacquer.

OPPOSITE
Classical forms, abstracted and made of whitewashed brick and hand-troweled plaster, are not simply tapping into traditions, they're helping to keep them alive.

LEFT
Whether the shapely end of a carved beam or the hand-sculpted profile of a column, architectural elements are a connection to the great traditions that preceded us.

OPPOSITE
Handcrafted ironwork has brought its own form of lyrical beauty to garden railings, gates, balustrades, and other architectural details through the centuries.

TIMELESSNESS

"The present was an egg laid by the past
that had the future inside its shell."
—ZORA NEALE HURSTON

Are we really so very different from the people who lived before us? It's true the things with which we surround ourselves are different, but fundamentally, isn't what we desire now the same as what our ancestors did then? The desire for security, to live surrounded by beauty, to be in nature, for our families to be cared for, all remain as steadfast to us today as they did to our ancestors. These basic desires are not tied to a particular time or culture but are affixed to that which is eternal. I've always said that I am much more interested in how we are the same as our ancestors than in how we are different from them.

It seems to me that creating architecture that appeals to our persistent human values is to create architecture that is timeless. It is architecture that goes beyond trends, is not predicated on a current fashion or today's state of the world. Rather, it aligns itself with deeper values, those that transcend time.

My goal is to create architecture that is enduring and sustainable; the buildings I design will achieve that only if the architecture is loved by my clients, and they are able to continue to find value in it into the indefinite future. I try to find ways of embedding character into the architecture that will allow people to continue to value it, continue to love it, and so assure its timelessness. Providing layers of meaning in the architecture is an important part of creating that assurance, and the style of the architecture is a key layer. Architectural "style" is really just a visual language, a method of communication. The language of style provides a way for our clients to make a personal connection to a particular culture, or a particular place. Early in the design process, I always work very closely with our clients to select a language for the architecture that has personal meaning for them.

RIGHT We took the vernacular of traditional architecture and its emphasis on connecting to the land, then updated it. It helped us express how we live in the present time in a way that somehow feels outside of time.

LEFT
Using a decidedly Mediterranean material palette of limestone, plaster, and wood beams (from salvaged barnwood) gave this new house a great sense of gracious timelessness.

OPPOSITE
The use of arched passages in Mediterranean cultures dates back centuries. Using them today, we evoked a feeling of traveling back in time to the silent passageways of age-old monasteries.

Selecting a particular style for their house might declare their bond to a singular place that has special meaning for them. And while the house's style is connected to that, at the same time it's more than that. I'm using the language of style to craft a story about their lives, creating an architecture particular to this family. For them, it might be a house that will always remind them of the warm feelings they had in a particular, special place. By connecting the dots of their life and using the house to bring them to the forefront, they will continue to love it and it will endure. This results in architecture that resonates on a higher plane, one that is personal and emotional, and not merely of the moment.

Another layer of meaning that brings value to the house is its use of materials. We appreciate life in such a rich and sensory way, and our houses can be designed and built to enhance our experiences. Our houses should invite our hands to pass over a handcrafted table as we move across a room. It should compel our eyes to dance over the array of design details in that same room, perhaps pausing at the 200-year-old antique door we salvaged and incorporated into the house. Salvaged elements can impart a timeless quality by entwining a contemporary house with the past. The sensual connections we have with the architecture appeal to our innate appreciation of beauty and reflect our deep connection to the natural world: these are timeless qualities. Textures, colors, and patterns all add enormous value to a house. Of course, buildings speak to us as sculptural objects, at the largest scale. But the details of hand-hewn elements, embellished textures of the vegetal or the floral, the moldings of interior millwork, or the undulating surface of hand-troweled plaster, all engage us at the fine scale, the human scale. When our architecture appeals to us in this way, at multiple scales, both large and small, it offers us another layer of meaning, one that speaks to us in the same way as nature: textures, colors, and patterns at multiple scales.

The final layer which I believe brings value to a home is its landscape. When architecture feels at home in its surroundings, at one with the landscape, it connects us to the eternal. As a contemporary classical architect, if my work only focused on designing period piece homes that emulate houses from a bygone era, I'd be neither achieving timelessness nor saying anything thoughtful about the present day. The language of traditional architecture needs to speak to how we live now, not 200 years ago, because while our core human qualities endure, our lifestyles change. The interiors of the houses I design express a well-considered use of language to address a modern lifestyle; it's embedded in the tradition of architecture, challenging its status as a contemporary home. Houses that address a way of living surpass fleeting trends.

Great architecture reaches out to us and gives us multiple reasons to love it. In this way, our connection to buildings is similar to a loving relationship with another person. We don't love just one thing about them, we love them as a whole. As we move through life together, we continue to discover new things to love, new reasons to want that person to stay just the way they are. Architecture should do the same thing, and it can. When it succeeds, it can connect us to something beyond ourselves.

OPPOSITE Bringing in water and fire through the courtyard plunge pool and loggia fireplace serves as a reminder of the eternal elements of the natural world.

OPPOSITE
& RIGHT
Close-ups of classical traditional elements that we abstracted, simplified, and made wholly unique to this location, house, and client. Though the redesign is fresh, its timeless feeling was created by referring to traditional prototypes without duplicating them.

LEFT
The arched opening, barnwood ceiling, and cozy sitting area overlooking the ocean, characteristics of the Mediterranean vernacular, make putting a date on this new house rather hard, while imagining it has existed there for generations is fairly easy.

OPPOSITE
I appreciate how working in traditional architecture lets me tap into a grand tradition while making it wholly relevant for today's lifestyle. It's about architecture moving out of the past, into the present, and outliving us in the future.

BEAUTY

"The sacred and the beautiful stand side by side, two doors that open onto a single space—and in that space we find our home."
—ROGER SCRUTON

When my children were young, we went on a family vacation to Sequoia National Park. As we hiked in a bit, the sounds took on a muffled thickness; hiking farther in, soon there were no other people around, and it was just us standing under a vast canopy of old trees. I remember watching them take it in, or trying to—the trees were so tall, and they were so small. But the thing I remember most was what I saw register on their faces . . . the experience of beauty. Innately, they knew what they were seeing was beautiful. I didn't have to teach them. It was part of their being. The ability to perceive beauty is embedded deep within our DNA. It's part of our human nature. There are many differences between us: the details of our physical appearance; our height, eye color, hair color, to name just a few; but I'm much more interested in the things we share. Our ability to perceive and be touched by beauty is one of these things.

Architecture can and should appeal to our rational, ordered, and philosophical minds. We can learn to see it through a cultural lens. But at the same time, it can directly touch our souls. Throughout my life, experiencing architecture has provided me with many "child in the forest" moments. No matter how often I've been to Frank Lloyd Wright's Guggenheim Museum in New York, each time I enter its foyer and stare upwards at the sweeping curve of its ramp and its soaring atrium, I am moved. The same is true for me at St. Peter's Basilica at the Vatican, where the simple act of gazing up at its dome touches me deeply. We have all had encounters like this. These kinds of extraordinary experiences seem to circumvent the rational mind and go straight into the subconscious.

Classical architecture seems particularly facile at providing both kinds of experiences. I can intellectually admire the Doric order, dive

RIGHT Being in service to our clients means finding every opportunity to give them access to the beauty of nature.

into its mathematical proportions and calming symmetries, but I can also simply walk into a classical building and let its beauty wash over me. Both are valid ways to explain the architecture, and both views are necessary for a full understanding.

My highest aspiration as an architect is to make people's lives better through the design of their homes. One vital way to do that is through beauty. For human beings, beauty is a necessity, as essential as food, water, and the air we breathe. It's there to remind us of the good, while offering itself to us as a counterbalance to life's chaos.

This is what a beautiful home has the potential to provide. I think my work is so fulfilling to me because I aim to understand our client's aspirations, and then incorporate them in the architecture of their house. Their home is the place where they live, feel safe, at peace, and most themselves; providing them with beauty is an important path to achieving this.

Nothing gives me greater happiness than having a client call up and say they woke up and walked into their living room where the light was falling across the floor in a beautiful way, and it caught something in the ceiling, and it just seemed to glow—and it was beautiful. Artists, painters, sculptors, architects, we all want our work to resonate with people. This is not a new idea or a novel desire; it's one that has consumed us forever. I believe that one of the keys to how we can achieve this is through beauty, the great unifier of people.

In beauty, I find hope. Through beauty, I am able to wonder at the mysteries of life.

Architecture is my portal to beauty.

OPPOSITE & RIGHT What provides beauty? Without question, it's the intersection of the architecture, nature's symmetry, and handcrafted detailing. And then there are those random flecks of gold in the pool tiles, shimmering in the deep blue water while evoking the stars above.

OPPOSITE
Encountering beauty as it unfolds in the landscape before us.

RIGHT
Through the entry foyer and out to the lush garden in back, architecture becomes a portal to nature's beauty, while restored ironwork provides fanciful details to further delight the eye.

OPPOSITE
Moments of beauty are everywhere to be found, both in nature and in the architecture that reflects it.

RIGHT
The contrast between the architecture's man-made shapes and the landscape's natural forms provides a backdrop to the view that never fails to inspire: sunset.

RIGHT &
FOLLOWING
From thoughtful proportions and a sense of place to traditional materials and timeless details, to the connection to nature and California, all elements come together to create a contemporary house whose beauty endures.

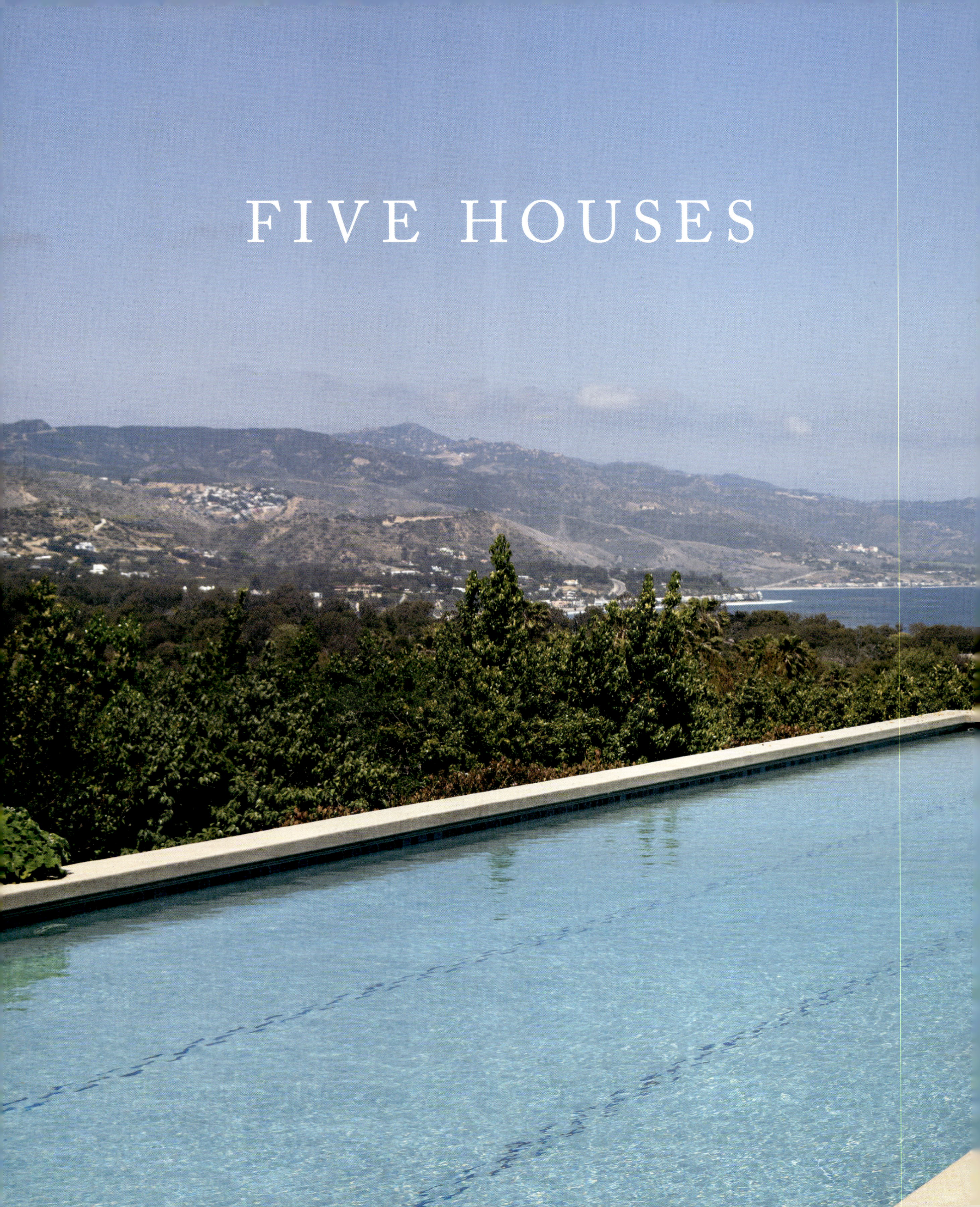

FIVE HOUSES

DUME DRIVE

Malibu, California

OPPOSITE
As seen through the gates to the entry courtyard, the home's front door reveals the strong central axis on which the house is aligned.

Driving into Malibu, a sign greets you that reads, "21 miles of scenic beauty"; it might be stating the obvious, but it might also be understating it. Along that strip of coastline the waves are perfect, the sand is soft, and rugged hills rise up and head inland. Beyond its varied topography, Malibu is a place with varied locales, and Point Dume is one of its most unique. I may be biased. I'm a fan of this notable point that juts out about three-quarters of a mile into the Pacific; its view of the arc of the Santa Monica Bay curve is one of my favorites. At night, when the lights of the city are on and the bay to the south shimmers, its nickname, the Queen's Necklace, is beautifully evident.

Aside from the view, the great appeal of Point Dume might be that it's a real neighborhood, with a genuine small-town vibe. The streets feel like country roads with ill-defined and ragged edges that go in a little here, out a little there. And while you won't see sidewalks, you might see horses, trotting along the road or across the landscape. This is Point Dume, low-key, lovely, and family-oriented. Oh, and yes, there's the beach, too, and for our clients, that was not insignificant. Native Angelenos, they craved an outdoor-oriented lifestyle and a property that would enable it. They yearned for a connection to the land and to the ocean. When they found it on Dume Drive, they reached out to us.

We dove into conversations about the kind of house they saw themselves residing in. We explored their aesthetics, discovered the language that spoke to them, learned what makes them happy. Then we zeroed in on the one word that would guide us throughout the years-long project: informal. Staying true to that word, we designed their 8,200-square-foot Spanish Colonial Revival house with no formal living room, because in this house, there is no formal living. Then we took the idea one step further and designed a house where the heart of the home isn't even *in* the home; rather, it's an outdoor room, a great loggia.

The moment you enter the front door, you look straight out the arched glass doors and into the loggia, the central space of the house. Everything filters into the covered loggia. The kitchen, dining room, family room, and the main stair hall all open onto it. While working on the design, I was inspired by the idea that I could take an outdoor, covered space and make it the focal point of the house. But as proud of that loggia as I am, I'm just

as proud of this home's interior architecture and the spaces that support this family.

The house has a complete wing on the south side devoted to a 25-by-75-foot great room. Serving three functions—cooking, dining, and leisure—in one big space, it addresses this client's notion of, and desire for, informal family living. It also allows us to bring in light from all sides, and make best use of the wind and ocean breezes that flow through this wing; they cool the house so thoroughly that although there is air conditioning, it's not really needed.

At the end of the family room, we placed a pointed Gothic arch, a shape I'm particularly fond of. This element has a long history in Mediterranean architecture. Though there are many other arched openings in the house, most are rounded; we reserved the Gothic arch for this special window that frames the magnificent view of the Santa Monica Bay to the south. In this way, the architecture speaks to us, whispering, "This vista is important . . . come and see."

Classical architecture does this kind of silent communicating so well, and in this traditional house, we took advantage of that beyond the arches. Though the house is relaxed and rambling, we embedded symmetries within it. The family can walk around their home's loose assemblage of form, and every once in a while be greeted by a symmetry; it's as if everything was once fuzzy, and at a special spot it's come sharply into view.

We employed this concept in the primary bedroom, which occupies the entire upper back of the house. Entering it, you're on the symmetrical center line, looking through to the private upper loggia. It's another way to connect our outdoor-centric clients to the view of nature and the ocean. It also let us fulfill a specific desire our client expressed to us: an intimate place to curl up and read a book. We designed a built-in sofa and enclosed it in a bay window that has a view of the Queen's Necklace.

We collaborated with Alana Homesley, a gifted interior designer. Her aesthetic and restrained palette worked so well here, and her vision, a bit more modern in feel, complements the architecture beautifully. The tilework you'll find in a vintage Spanish-style home from the 1920s, which is the inspiration for this house, is usually exuberant color; instead, Alana chose a hand-cut Moroccan tile for the stairs. It's decorative, but not overly fussy; it suits the style perfectly, and is also unique to this house. Like us, she was not interested in duplicating the 1920s style but instead sought to use the language of that era's Mediterranean architecture with a modern sensibility.

The success of this house is revealed in a particularly Malibu kind of story. In 2018, a devastating wildfire tore through Malibu. Our client tried in vain to get news about the condition of his family's house. Had it survived, or had it succumbed to the random destruction of the fire? But Point Dume was completely blocked off. Only emergency vehicles could enter. When he could no longer cope with not knowing, he hired a boat, whose captain took him around the point and got him as close to the shoreline as possible. Donning a wetsuit, he dove into the ocean, swam to the beach, and hiked up the path to his still-standing house. My team and I were shocked when he told us this story; we were also incredibly moved by the love he and his family feel for their house. What would you do for the love of your house? I've thought about it many times.

OPPOSITE Warm wood details, terra-cotta tiles, and smooth plaster, quintessential elements of Spanish Colonial architecture, are captured in Southern California's radiant sunlight.

FOLLOWING The main house level gently cascades to the pool terrace, which we envisioned as another room of the house. Imagining it this way let us create a house as gracious as it is spacious, allowing our client to live a "home as resort" lifestyle.

BEFORE THEY PASS AWAY
JIMMY NELSON
YAYOI KUSAMA
INFINITY MIRRORS

PREVIOUS
I conceived this loggia as the heart of the house. Under its antique terra-cotta vaulting, where each individual rib is hand-carved, the central space becomes another opportunity for family gathering and living.

LEFT
By contrasting the texture of the wood with the smoothness of the hand-troweled plaster, we not only impart a dynamic quality to the architecture but also provide a great variety of aesthetic experiences.

LEFT
Traditional architecture can adapt to modern living effortlessly. Here, it's done through a great room, where kitchen, dining, and living all happen in one place.

ABOVE
Every beam of the house was hand-hewn on-site, executed by local craftspeople.

FOLLOWING
Incorporating a salvaged carved beam in the range hood provides a heightened sense of history.

2

PREVIOUS
There's a great tradition in Spanish architecture of having beautiful corner fireplaces, often in the bedroom. We tap into this tradition here to maintain the room's central focus of the broad bay window, with its sweeping view of the coastline.

LEFT
Salvaged antique doors lead into the primary bathroom, where an Asian rug brings the space lovely softness, texture, and color.

OPPOSITE
I love all the textures and materiality of this space; every surface has an engaging quality to it.

FOLLOWING
The loggia at twilight with its view of the pool. In the distance, Santa Monica Bay's "Queen's Necklace" is quietly beginning to shimmer.

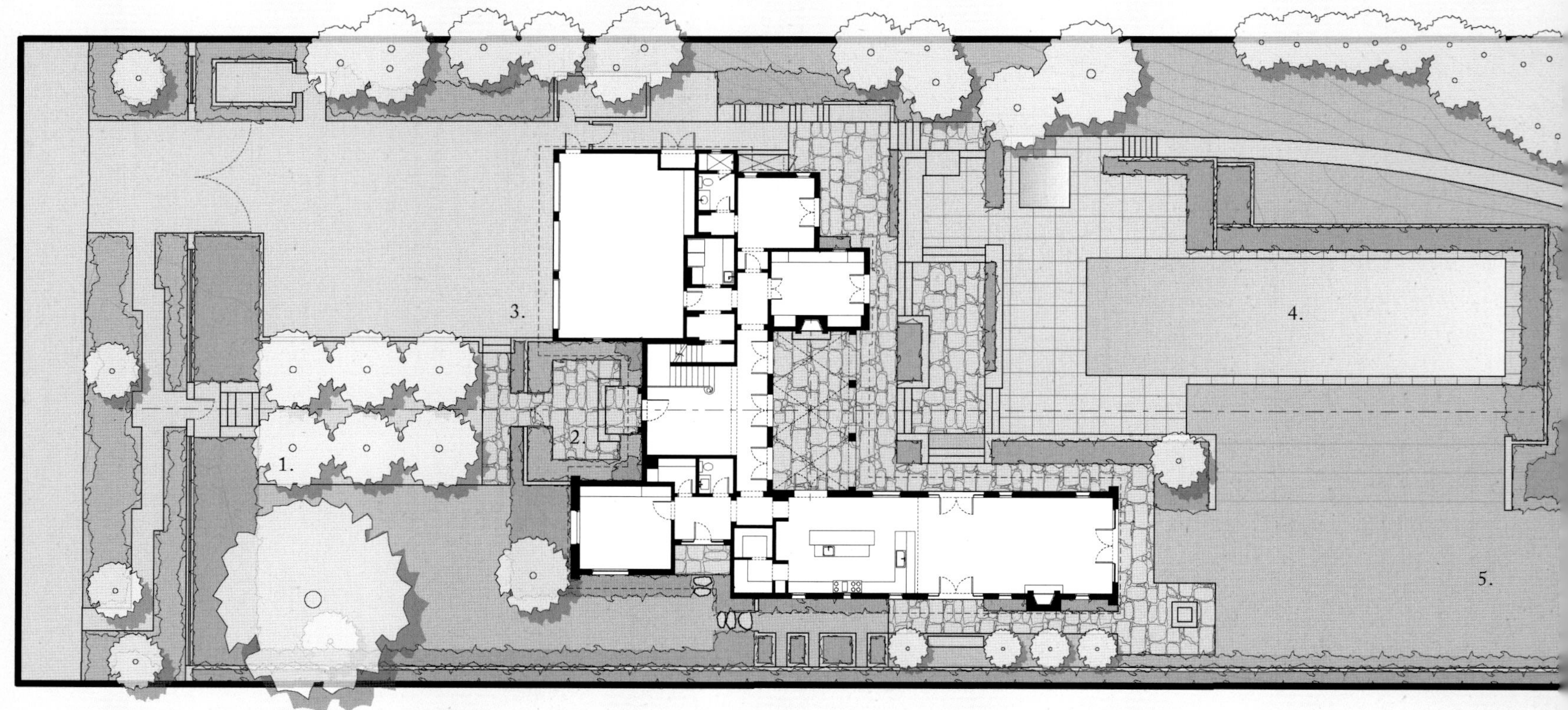

SITE PLAN

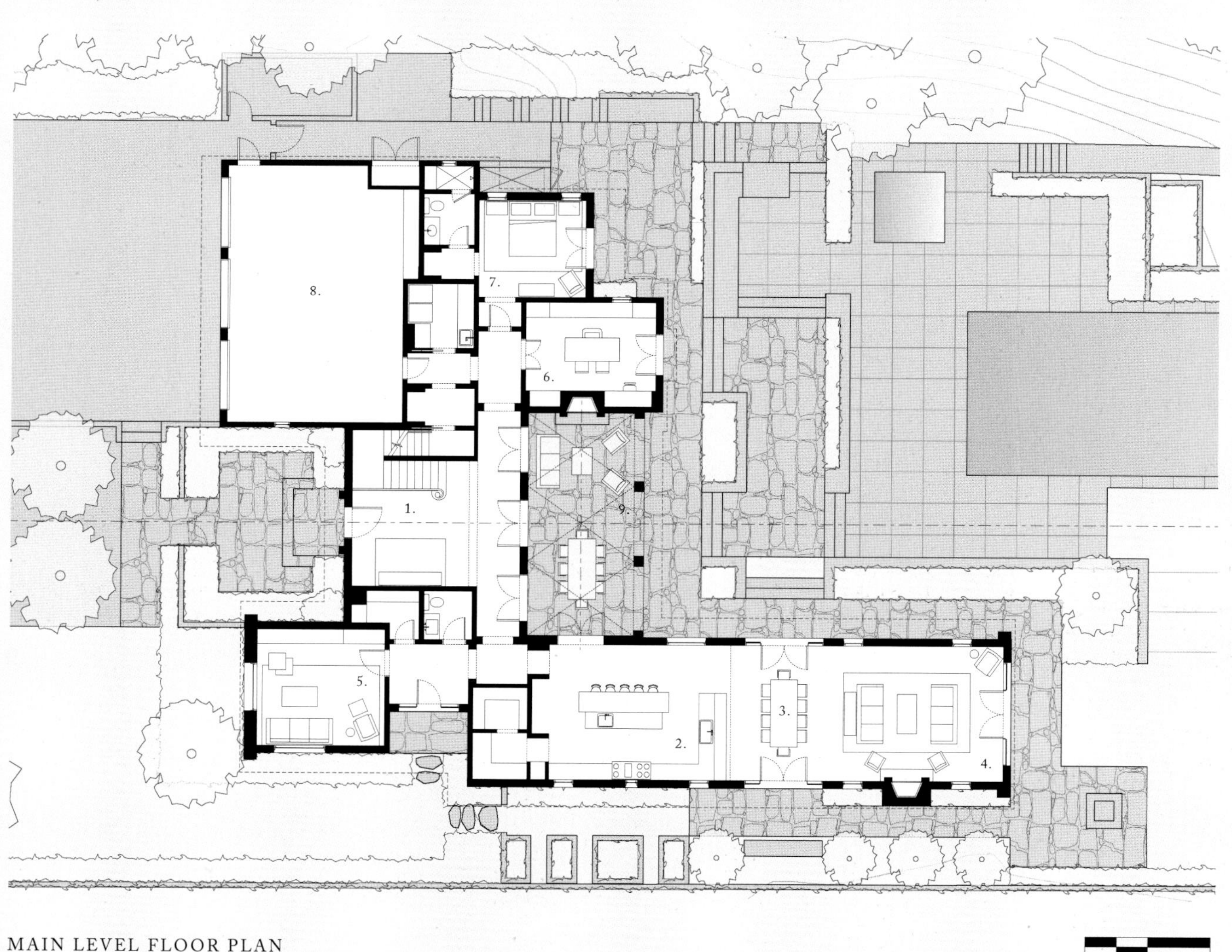

MAIN LEVEL FLOOR PLAN

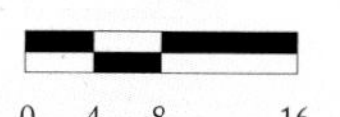

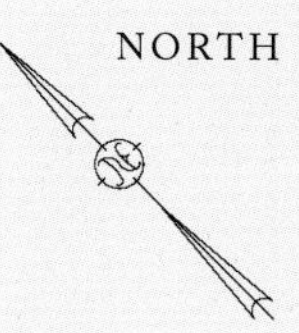

0 8 16 32

SITE LEGEND

1 Entry Allée
2 Entry Courtyard
3 Motor Court
4 Pool
5 Great Lawn

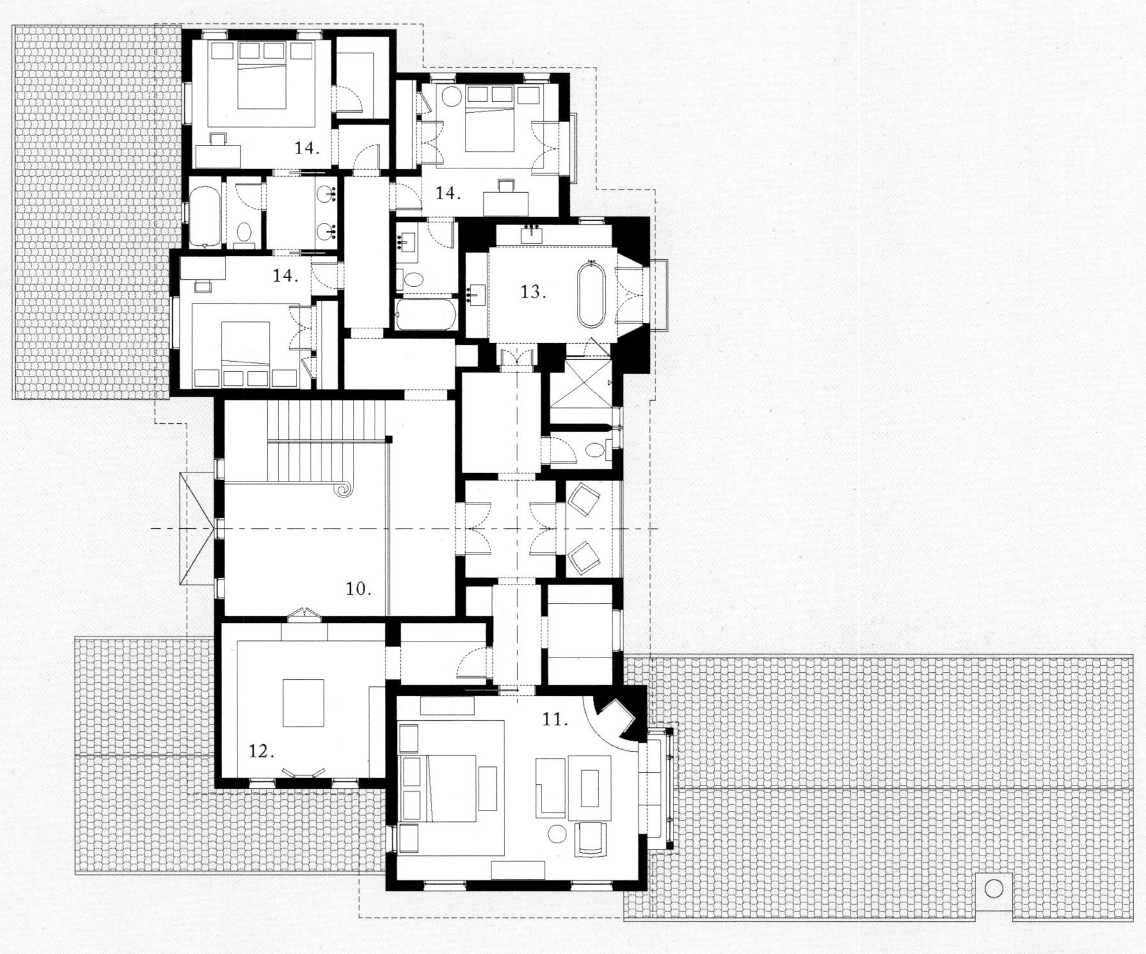

SECOND LEVEL FLOOR PLAN

0 4 8 16

PLAN LEGEND

1 Foyer
2 Kitchen
3 Dining Room
4 Family Room
5 Den
6 Office
7 Guest Bedroom
8 Garage
9 Loggia
10 Upper Foyer
11 Primary Bedroom
12 Primary Closet
13 Primary Bathroom
14 Bedroom

OLD AGOURA

Agoura Hills, California

The Temple of Apollo in Delphi, Greece, is on my list of places to visit, and not only for the expected reason: seeing the ruins of a perfectly proportioned, classically structured Greek temple. What also calls to me is a quote inscribed on its side, "Know Thyself." As maxims go, I relate strongly to this one, and so, how wonderful to work with the clients of this Old Agoura house. Know thyself? They did, thoughtfully and thoroughly. They knew their values, and knew they wanted a house that reflected them. The great joy of our work was to visually express those values through the architecture.

Their awareness of themselves, as a family and as individuals, led to a specific list of things that was important to them. Three things were high on the list: an informal lifestyle, sports, and knowledge. Designing their house to those values meant another nod to the Greeks, this time to their passion for mythology.

OPPOSITE
A gracious, welcoming entry porch in the traditional American style conjures up feelings of what it means to be "home."

We created our own myth for the architecture of this project in Old Agoura, basing it loosely on American rural architecture. Imprinting our sense of "farmhouse" as a starting point, we took the style, fine-tuned it for the landscape, and made it work for California, enabling it to connect to the landscape in a more fluid way. Our myth tells the story of an original little farmhouse sitting on an expansive six acres with horses roaming the canyon's soft hills. Over the years, the farmhouse saw many additions as it was passed from one generation to the next. This generative myth gave us a purpose and a framework for determining what form the house would take. Eventually, the myth did the same for the interior design, expressed so beautifully by my talented friend Joe Lucas.

Key to any good myth is a good challenge, and this project had one. Though we had the freedom to place the house wherever we wanted, site analysis led us to the top of the property, where commanding views and breezes come from the south and west. This is where we met our challenge . . . actually, seven of them: seven California live oak trees, prominent and protected by law. Many conversations, debates, and scrapped ideas eventually led us to a design that is embedded with and around the oaks. Once we reconciled the floor levels of the house with the height of the surrounding trees, we were ready to address the challenge of turning values into a built form.

LEFT
The architecture is carefully aligned with the tradition of American farmhouses. It's seen in the bilateral symmetry, the wood clapboard siding, and the well-proportioned dormers.

ABOVE
Just inside the entry, dogs do the welcoming, or maybe just enjoy the view.

The client's desire for informal living led to our decision to forgo a formal and separate dining room. Instead, we incorporated it into daily life via the creation of the "Great Hall." Spanning the entire back of the house, and running down the center, the Great Hall is one part living room, one part dining room, with both parts having identical fireplaces facing each other from across the space. Between them is an intentionally unfurnished space. Acting as a visual and physical pathway, it's an allée from the entrance to the outdoors, drawing visitors toward the back, the landscape, and the view.

Adjacent to the Great Hall to the west are the family room, breakfast room, and kitchen. We looked back to our original farmhouse mythology when designing this private family area and created a fictive narrative about an old barn in need of some dedicated TLC. We rehabbed it and made a connection to the existing house. The space has trusses of hand-hewn timber that start at the kitchen, then march along to the family room. Reaching heights of fifteen feet at the ridge, the trusses create a lofty space. The family area runs across the back, where it opens out, through broad windows and French doors, to the spacious, covered veranda. Graciously scaled for comfort, and easily accommodating permanent outdoor seating and dining, the veranda is used year-round, taking full advantage of the area's temperate climate.

Beyond the veranda lies much of the expression of the second value: sports. The husband was a former college baseball player, so it wasn't too surprising that this was important and made the list. But it wasn't important just to him; it was equally so to his wife and their three children, all very athletic, all very outdoorsy. We started by indulging some sports fantasies: a batting cage and practice area lie to the northwest, a soccer field to the north, and to the west is an all-purpose yard that accommodates a jungle gym, badminton, and more. Another key sports zone is the pool area. Located farthest down the hill, it is gated, private, quiet, and has its own outdoor fireplace.

Exposure to knowledge was the third value we addressed. Through our conversations, we understood that it held enormous meaning and significance for them, so much so that we committed ourselves to deliberately shaping the house to underscore the value. Our approach to the library did just that, while also helping to form our thoughts about the bedroom wing.

You cannot avoid the library, and our clients didn't want it to be hidden. Rather than design it as a separate room, we used the library as a circulation space; you have to walk through it to get to the bedroom wing. We created an open walkway along the side of the library, an aisle which ensured everyone's presence in the library every day. Passing through it is something of a lovely amble. The room's large windows offer a view of the largest of the old, protected oaks; its beautiful fireplace makes the room cozy, plus, the color Joe chose for its walls, a eucalyptus green, is rich and inviting. Incorporating a family library—making it central to family life so that everyone, children and parents, are encouraged to read—I feel, is one of the greatest triumphs of this house.

In many ways, each day up here is a kind of homecoming for this family. Our client grew up in the town, and though she moved away for a time, she knew the hills, knew the roads, knew that the one-lane bridge over the creek doesn't just slow traffic, but also time. For the whole family, their home embodies their past, what made them who they are, and anticipates who they look forward to becoming.

PREVIOUS Large and accommodating, the scale of the rear veranda is perfect for a family.

LEFT Sunlight on the property is magical. The rolling hills that ascend west to the Santa Monica Mountains glow a vibrant gold when dry and become verdant green when the rainy season arrives.

RIGHT
Serene interiors by the talented Joe Lucas are not intended to shock so much as to soothe. The quiet, soft blue-gray paneling in the foyer is so calming, and also so American in the way it evokes the old Federal houses of the east.

FOLLOWING
Like a great drawing room in an old European estate, but with a relaxed, farmhouse character, nothing feels forced in the Great Hall; everything feels gracious.

LIVING IN
Richard Meier

INTERIOR DECORATION
Interiors

The GARDENS of BUNNY MELLON
AMERICAN ORIGINALS

PREVIOUS
Some rooms always elicit the same response from me. In this breakfast room, with its comfortable scale and transom windows bringing the outside architecture in, the feeling is serene and calm.

OPPOSITE & RIGHT
The golden Belgian linen curtains engage in a buoyant dialogue with the Fromental wall covering. Hand-painted on tea paper, it's one of the wondrous choices Joe Lucas made that allow this room sing.

FOLLOWING LEFT & RIGHT
In a house with many grandly scaled rooms, we envisioned the library as a cozy, denlike space for privacy and retreat. The richly colored eucalyptus-green walls and fireplace of fieldstone rubble with a simple wood mantel make it easy to imagine reading the afternoon away.

HANDCRAFTED MODERN
TILE MAKES THE ROOM
GOOD DESIGN FROM HEATH CERAMICS
THE ILIAD OF HOMER
OBERTO GILI HOME SWEET HOME
WHISTLER

LEFT
To give the large space a rehabbed barn feel, I used white tongue-and-groove siding as a reference to American farmhouse interiors, and designed the elliptical, bowstring arch trusswork to emulate traditional barn framing.

ABOVE
Detail of the copper lantern and the family room's beautiful trusswork.

LEFT
Our client requested a place where she could prep meals and do dishes, all while watching her kids play right outside; the large window over the sink was our response to her loving desire.

OPPOSITE
Two islands inhabit the kitchen: one, big and functional in the center, and the second, a built-in buffet, designed for extra storage and for the client to lay out an easily accessed meal.

FOLLOWING LEFT
High clerestory windows flood the bedroom with a soft, lovely light.

FOLLOWING RIGHT
At the top of the stairs, an antique bench offers a quiet moment of pause.

LEFT
Big, broad, and accommodating, the veranda's architecture makes the exact kind of response it should make for the setting: providing shade and shelter from the ever-present sun.

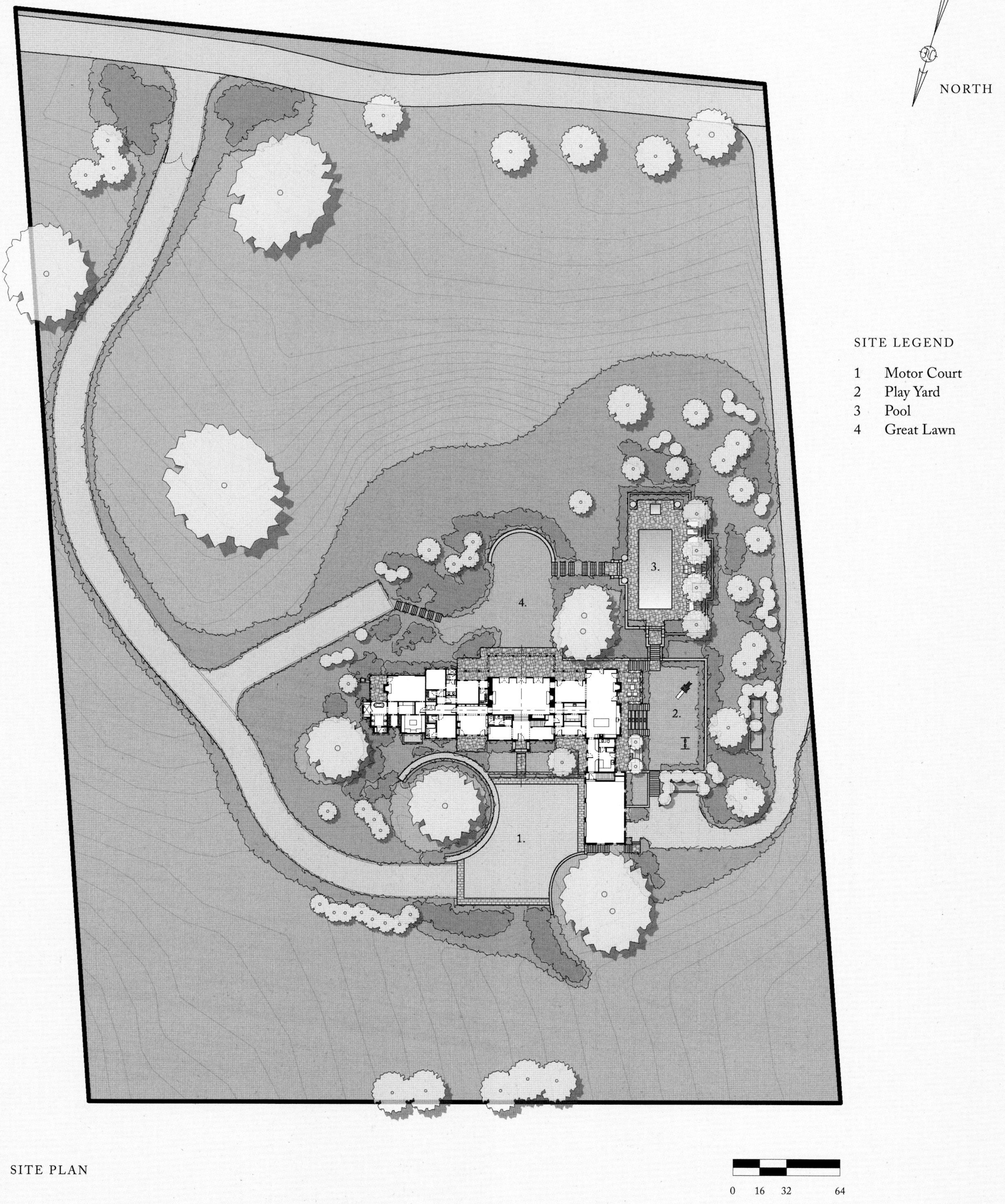

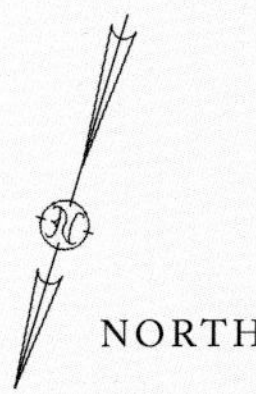

SITE LEGEND

1 Motor Court
2 Play Yard
3 Pool
4 Great Lawn

SITE PLAN

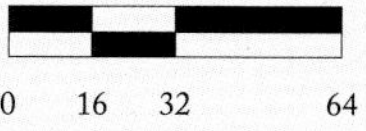

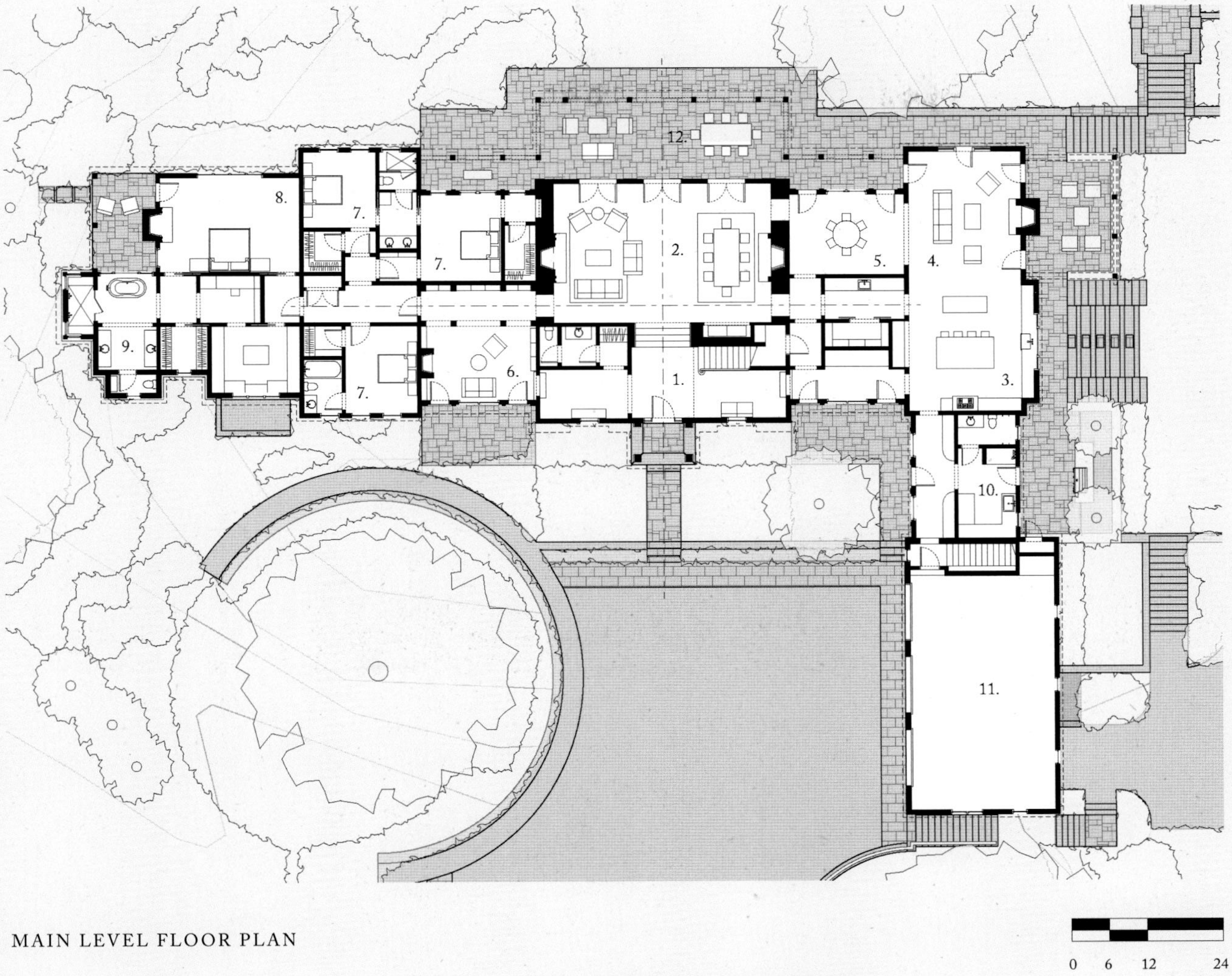

MAIN LEVEL FLOOR PLAN

0 6 12 24

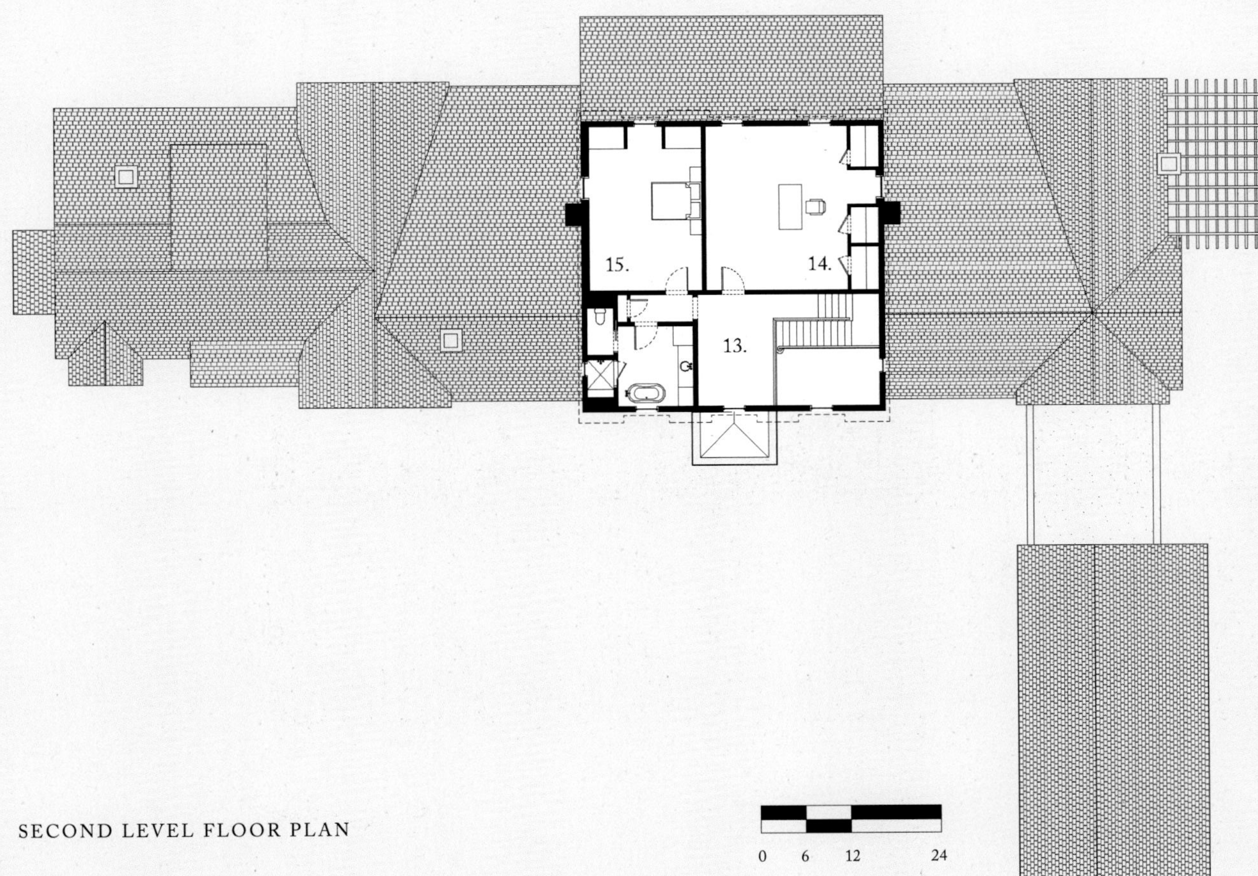

SECOND LEVEL FLOOR PLAN

0 6 12 24

PLAN LEGEND

1 Foyer
2 Great Hall
3 Kitchen
4 Family Room
5 Breakfast Room
6 Family Library
7 Bedroom
8 Primary Bedroom
9 Primary Bathroom
10 Laundry
11 Garage
12 Veranda
13 Upper Foyer
14 Office
15 Guest Bedroom

PARRA GRANDE

Montecito, California

For most of my life, the romance of California has held me captive. Perhaps one of its strongest and most enduring draws lies in Santa Barbara and neighboring Montecito. Snugly situated between the Pacific Ocean and the Santa Ynez Mountains, it's hard not to find the area alluring. And that is *before* I take in the Santa Barbara sandstone, in evidence nearly everywhere. From churches and bell towers to bridges and gates, and of course, to the glorious Mission Santa Barbara, this rough and rubbly rock is omnipresent. Happily so for me, because whenever my eyes rest on its textured surface, I see beauty. Skilled masons have been chiseling those golden, soft tan surfaces for centuries. Our Montecito project allowed me to carry on the tradition of using this material in its natural locale, as well as to humbly follow in the footsteps of two residential architects I greatly admire: George Washington Smith and Wallace Neff. Over a century ago, both used the same sandstone for their remarkable Mediterranean-style houses.

OPPOSITE
Grapevines grow over and through the pergola's trellised roof, while in the distance, cascading water spills over a sculptural fountain featuring dancing figures.

This house, however, is *not* rooted in the Mediterranean. With the simple form of its gabled roofs, it blends California Ranch style with local agricultural precedent. What enhances the blend is the house's connection to the landscape. Not only does it speak loudly to me of my romantic notion of California, but it also makes this a landscape project as much as an architectural one.

The topography of the site is dramatic and complicated: it is all sloping, the sole exception being the east side of the property, where you find the only piece of flat land, and thus, the main house. We strove to take full advantage of all the usable areas of the land we could find; once found, we incorporated them into a wide variety of places for our client to visit and enjoy. There are sitting areas, outdoor dining spots, and a set of winding stairs that arrive at a terrace with its own fireplace. There's a pergola, with benches, leading to stairs that drop down to a vegetable and rose garden. There's a sloping meadow, and across it we dispersed a mix of wildflowers; every spring the field erupts in color. And finally, because the Los Padres National Forest embraces the environs, there had to be a hammock in the woods.

Not surprisingly, we found many ways to use Santa Barbara sandstone: as a sturdy base; for walls, columns, and terraces; and for the numerous fireplaces. Its presence makes the house

feel embedded in the landscape. We even used it on the walls of the unusual, "natural" swimming pool we designed. Ecologically sound and using no harsh chemicals, the pool's filtration takes place naturally, functioning almost like a fish tank, with pumps pulling the water through the gravel lining the bottom. The swimming area is in the middle, surrounded by a wall that comes within an inch or so of the surface, keeping out aquatic plants and fish that aid in the cleansing of the water. It gives the feel of an old-fashioned swimming hole in the forest, which allowed us to meld the pool with the landscape in a way that felt natural and indigenous.

The other major factor of the landscape design was the preservation of over forty native oak trees. By incorporating them into our plans, our client became their stewards for the next generation. Within this oak forest, our work was very deliberate. The structures on the site comprise a main house and its satellite buildings: a pool house, a guesthouse, and a charming little gardening shed, a prefabricated building that we dressed up by adding the same roofing, and giving it a little cupola. We thought, "why shouldn't it, like every other structure on the property, have its own presence?"

Inside, the house is a true blending of ranch vernacular, with a slightly more modern sensibility. Where it seemed appropriate, we opened the house out to the landscape, usually with glass. It's there in the great room, which combines the family room, kitchen, and breakfast banquette. It's there in our decision to avoid overhead cabinets in the kitchen, opting instead to keep everything low so we could have that big, beautiful wall of windows.

The interior detailing is fairly humble, not overly fancy or embellished with a lot of decorative flourishes. Instead there are simple moldings and unadorned, Shaker-style millwork. The ceilings' exposed rafters are painted white, recalling how old ranch buildings were always painted back in the day. Walls are often tongue and groove; its unpretentious, rural feel works beautifully for the home, and became a theme we played out throughout the house. Starting immediately in the entry area, the tongue and groove continues along the downstairs hall before moving upstairs, where it lines the hallway leading to the bedroom wing. The stair tower, our nod to Mission Santa Barbara, is also tongue and groove and takes you to the upper level, but then extends above it. During the day it brings in light; at night its lights glow like a beacon.

The process of designing this house was an iterative one. The landscape was at the table right from the beginning, allowing us to go back and forth from the architecture to the landscape throughout. I worked alongside our incredibly talented landscape director

PREVIOUS As you enter the motor court, the house presents itself: graciously scaled entry porch, welcoming front door, and to the right, a stair tower, my small nod to the bell towers of the California missions.

LEFT Olive trees lend shade to a lavender-scented walk to the porch. Roofing of corrugated zinc, a reference to central California's agricultural barns, doesn't just add texture, it also doesn't rust.

Michael McGowan, and as the architecture took form I saw how it would engage the landscape. Then Michael explored ways for the landscape to inform the buildings. All along, we worked hard to make sure one discipline wasn't being reactive to the other, but that they functioned as an integrated whole. That was critical here; the client knew this was a special piece of land, and wanted the house to capture the ethos of its locale. As a result, he and his family felt deeply connected to the property.

The home has become a family compound for children and grandchildren who come from near and far, and where arrival often means a noisy welcome from chickens roaming freely outside their coop. Inside, the greeting is a little more serene, with fresh cut roses and wildflowers in vases, citrus fruits in bowls. It's their headquarters, their home base, the place where the whole family can convene, decamp, and enjoy a little of the romance and a lot of the bliss of life in California.

RIGHT Santa Barbara sandstone forms the connective tissue of the stone walls throughout Montecito, and it is a standout here as well. Large stones fit tightly together like the pieces of a puzzle. Local stone masons know the tradition, dating back to the early 1900s, and uphold it with pride.

LEFT
Comfortably scaled and furnished, the veranda's sitting areas are accessed through broad folding doors. The coloration of the Sweetwater flagstone paving perfectly complements the Santa Barbara sandstone walls.

FOLLOWING
Blending classical architecture with the California Ranch style, the symmetrical pool house is carefully aligned with the natural swimming pool, which unfolds like a carpet in front of it. Large sliding doors in the front and back offer views of, and access to, a wildflower meadow beyond.

RIGHT
White painted beams with white tongue-and-groove decking make this a cheerful space for eating and unwinding. Bright and airy, the room engages beautifully with the garden.

LEFT
Warm wood walls create a cozy breakfast nook, whose built-in banquette seats six to eight comfortably. Paying homage to symmetry, we designed two windows: the left looks outside; the right looks inside to a vestibule with a desk.

RIGHT
Not wanting to obscure the allée of olive trees flourishing outside the windows, we eliminated overhead cabinets and built them below instead. Interiors by M. Elle tap into a traditional aesthetic but are freshened for a modern lifestyle.

RIGHT
At the top of the stairs there's a cozy family retreat complete with a writing desk for two. The lovely dormered space is made even lovelier thanks to the beautiful tree just outside the window, and beyond it, a view of the Pacific.

LEFT
The transparent gray-stained finish of the primary suite reveals the warmth of the wood. It's one piece of an overall calming feel. The fireplace is another. Its Santa Barbara sandstone, a highlight of the exterior, brings beauty into this bedroom.

FOLLOWING
A Greek temple form is reimagined here in a ranch vernacular, making the room's beautiful symmetry just magical. Adding to the magic is a decades-old sycamore standing guard at the end of the pool.

AIR and SPACE MUSEUM
Paintings for the Future
O'KEEFFE Visions of Hawai'i

Better Than Before
WASHINGTON
RON CHERNOW
MONSOON

SITE LEGEND

1 Motor Court
2 Orchard
3 Rose Garden
4 Vegetable Garden
5 Potting Shed and Chicken Coop
6 Dining Terrace
7 Play Lawn
8 Fireplace Terrace
9 Meadow
10 Pool House
11 Natural Swimming Pool

SITE PLAN

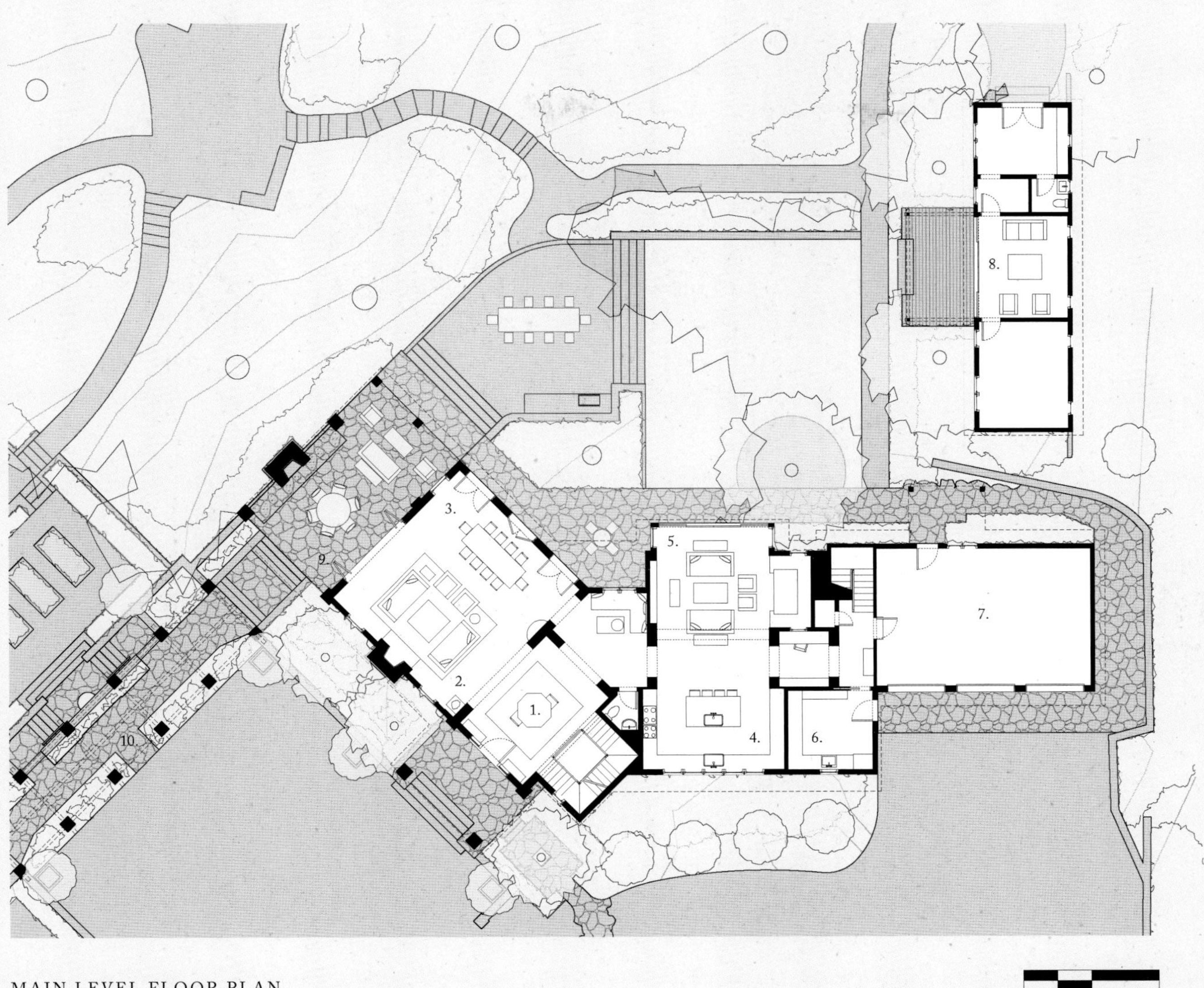

MAIN LEVEL FLOOR PLAN

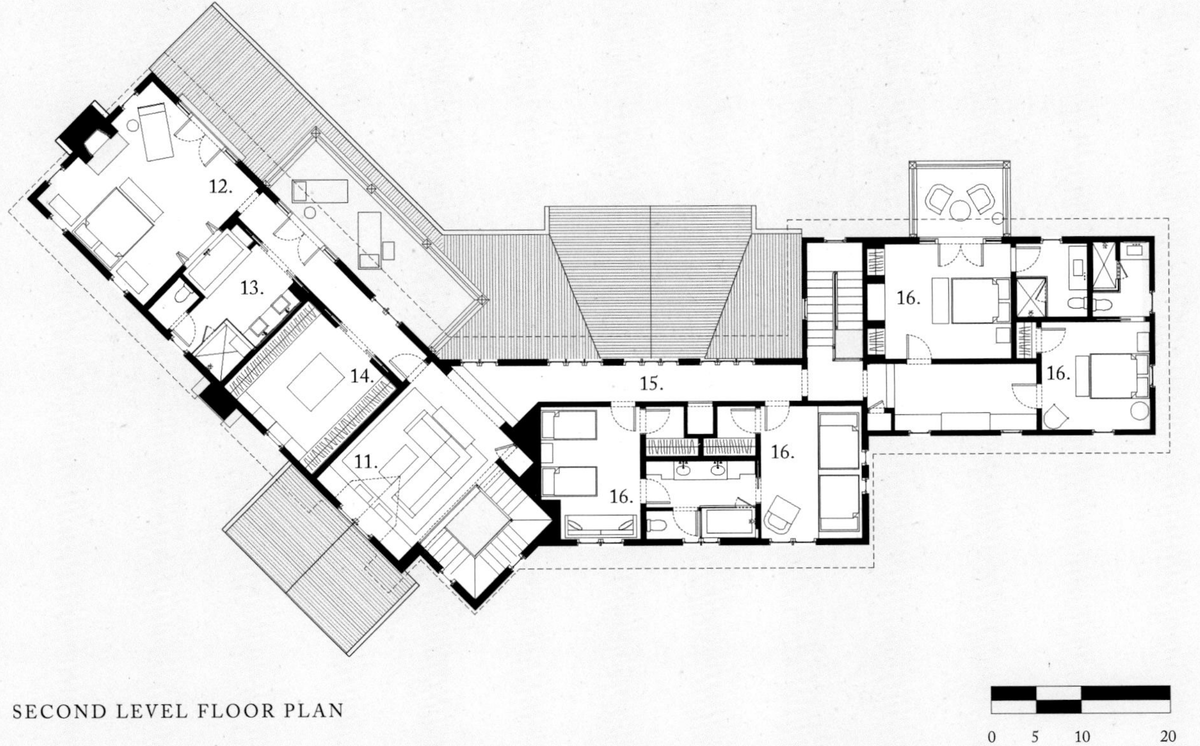

SECOND LEVEL FLOOR PLAN

PLAN LEGEND

1 Foyer
2 Living Room
3 Dining Room
4 Kitchen
5 Family Room
6 Laundry
7 Garage
8 Guesthouse
9 Veranda
10 Pergola
11 Retreat
12 Primary Bedroom
13 Primary Bathroom
14 Primary Closet
15 Gallery
16 Bedroom

STONE CANYON

Bel Air, California

Architecture encompasses such a varied range of components, all of which I enjoy diving into deeply: history, mathematics, problem solving, creativity, precision, and even a touch of psychology. Yet, perhaps more than anything, I see architecture as a profession of hope: listening to a client's hopes for how they want to live in their house, and, in return, offering hope that what they want will, in fact, be possible. For this remodel of a house built in the 1930s, the hopes were clear: improve functionality and provide amenities the house didn't offer. High on the list was a proper dining room, a roomy, comfortable primary bedroom, and a large, functional kitchen.

Remodels present us with a different set of challenges that our new-build projects do not. When working from scratch, we make the rules, establish the language, and have more of a blank slate in front of us. Not so with a remodel, where we're presented with an existing context and a slate that is already filled. My team and I derive enormous satisfaction from taking a project designed by others and putting our stamp on it. There's another side to it too, which comes back to hope, or perhaps, the lack of it.

OPPOSITE
Classical elements come together in the carefully proportioned front porch: voussoirs of brick, slenderized Tuscan columns, and, of course, symmetry, all lend themselves to the house's warm sense of invitation.

Clients often have lower expectations for a remodel. Knowing they're dealing with an existing building, they approach their project with an air of resignation and the belief that only through significant compromises will they get what they want from their home. I love proving them wrong. Doing that means first challenging preexisting notions about compromises in remodels, and then, as we aspire to do in all our work, exceeding expectations. This project achieved these goals admirably.

Bel Air's Stone Canyon Road winds its way north from Sunset Boulevard, climbing the steep mountains above Beverly Hills. It's also an old road, and because of that I suspected we might be dealing with a vintage "builder's home," the kind that was typical of houses built in and around 1930s Los Angeles. Extremely well-designed and well-proportioned architecturally, and full of simple detailing, this quiet house proved to be a solid example of its genre. However, multiple unfortunate additions that had been made over the decades didn't meet our client's modern lifestyle, so we worked with interior designer Windsor Smith, setting out to address each need and every hope.

We focused our attention on the two arenas of landscape and architecture, and quickly made the decision to have landscape drive and architecture ride shotgun. Given the house's topography, it's hard to imagine it could have been any other way, for while the site had the room we needed, the backyard was, essentially, one large hill. The design had to be clever, not only in how it made effective use of all the land, but doing so in ways that were graceful and aesthetically pleasing. Terracing the hill provided the answer we sought. Creating three usable levels allowed the client to recoup valuable useable outdoor space, and allowed us to do a complete reworking of the existing house and to create a major addition.

The lowest terrace of the backyard is level with the house's kitchen, dining room, and public spaces. We pushed out, dug out, built a retaining wall, and gave them the extra space and amenities they desired: a stately lawn, fireplace, pergola, outdoor kitchen, and a sitting area with television and entertainment access.

Up next, the second level is accessed via meandering stairs that run along both sides of the house. You arrive at the pool, guesthouse, and a pergola with seating. This terrace level engages the primary bedroom extension, allowing the client to walk directly out of the second-story bedroom and to the pool. Even on the second floor of the house, they remain connected to the land. Too often that is not the norm, and getting to the second level means disconnecting from the landscape. Here, the space has the feel of a private indoor-outdoor sanctuary.

Heading to the third level you pass through a garden portal which leads you alongside the guesthouse, and then lands you at the sports terrace with basketball and pickleball courts. Sitting at the top of the property, the courts are tucked up against the hill and in their own world. Looking up from the house, no courts or nets are visible, just bits of lovely architectural details, the hill, and nature.

With the landscaping addressed, architecture moved into greater focus. We love a good gabled entry porch, and for this house, the one we designed gives the traditional Colonial its appropriate, classical welcoming moment. The door is blue, chosen by the interior designer Windsor Smith to match the steely blue eyes of the client, and while it is the first hint of what is to come, a visitor is certainly not prepared for what is revealed. Upon entering, your eye is drawn to the astonishing deep blue color of the dining room, whose high gloss lacquer is on all the surfaces, enveloping the walls and the ceiling. It's visually stunning, an almost surreal moment. We reclaimed the room from its previous life as a formal, little-used living room to create a much loved and much used dining space.

The kitchen, another complete reinvention of an existing space, was high on their list of hopes. A swinging door opens onto a room we designed in collaboration with Windsor's vision of glamour, which called for cool gray tones, marble countertops, and gold fittings and fixtures. We added the large picture window, giving the client a view of their new terraced landscape, as well as the beautiful and bountiful nature found in the hills of Bel Air.

We also used the kitchen as a way to straddle the old and the new via a large, multifunctional, ten-foot-wide arched passage. It didn't just create a fluid connection between the kitchen and the family and breakfast rooms, it did so while addressing modern-day needs within the more traditional language of the house. We even extracted pragmatic purposes from the arch by installing, into its great depth, pantry storage and a small writing desk.

One thing I love about a traditional house is the sense of expectation I have walking from room to room. The desire to give the client that experience informed the next part of the remodel. From the family room, you pass through a barn door to reach the adult lounge of the house; cozy, with comfortable, conversational seating, the space has a decidedly nightclub, speakeasy feel to it. The journey can end there, or take you beyond. Descending three steps brings you to the wine room. With black lacquer walls and a glass table with polished brass accents, the space is as easy to enjoy as the contents that line its walls.

Other architectural transformations occurred on the second floor. We designed three rooms for the three children, and a kids' space for homework and fun. However, the most extensive changes involved reconfiguring the entire primary suite. Completely occupying the back portion of the house, it includes a gym on one end and the bedroom on the other. The middle is anchored by the new primary bathroom.

We strive to make every bathroom more than utilitarian. We feel that it's just as important for them to be beautiful architectural experiences. Here, that was achieved by looking through an arched portal into a framed moment of perfect symmetry, the bathtub placed carefully in the center as if it were a piece of sculpture.

From the outside, the house may appear to be typically Colonial, but this isn't your grandmother's Colonial. Though aspects of the interiors remind us of those Colonial houses from the past, this house addresses the glamour of old Hollywood in a very modern, very current, Los Angeles way. One of the goals in every remodel we do is to give the resulting project a unified feel, so it feels consistent, has one point of view, is a complete environment. By optimizing the landscape, and amplifying the original great architecture of the house, the clients came away with all the amenities they wanted, and with very few compromises made, their hopes were fulfilled.

PREVIOUS Brickwork and a denticulated stringcourse divide and balance the house's facade. Amid the grays of the slate roof and gravel motor court, the blue door is a beckoning beacon.

OPPOSITE For the true center-hall Colonial we envisioned, we designed a proper entry, complete with an elegant transom window above the front door.

RIGHT
Creating a space that functions as a reception lounge meant removing a wall, then a door, then breaking it all wide open. Today, guests come in, sit, and relax, and if they have the inclination and the talent, they'll even play the piano.

FOLLOWING
Elegance meets surrealism when two traditional chairs, amid a cool gray palette, welcome us into an exotic world of color and mystery. The checkerboard floor emphasizes the moment of transition.

PREVIOUS
LEFT & RIGHT
A 15-foot-long dining table makes entertaining a joyful experience in Windsor Smith's exuberant and surprising interior. The art collection, eclectic and thought-provoking, is the perfect pairing for the space.

RIGHT
The broad elliptical archway was designed to be thick enough for storage, but also to act as a fluid connection between the breakfast room and kitchen.

FOLLOWING
In days past, kitchens were designed to be behind the scenes, but that's not how we live today; we designed this kitchen to be in the forefront of family life. The gold fixtures add an alluring touch.

colgin
2004
Guigal
Cote Rotie
2008
SAINT-ÉMILION

PREVIOUS
A grotto-like wine cellar and tasting room is reached only after passing through several rooms, heightening the anticipation of arrival to this stunning destination.

ABOVE
The elliptical arch, thematic throughout the house's architectural language, was also used here in the primary bath.

RIGHT
Peaceful, contemplative, and very intentionally restrained, the primary suite's cool blue-grays provide a beautiful contrast with the bright greens of the landscaping.

RIGHT
A pergola provides shade to the sitting area, while use of the same slenderized Tuscan columns of the front porch provides a consistent theme.

FOLLOWING LEFT
White surfaces accentuate the play of light and shadow on traditional detailing.

FOLLOWING RIGHT
The family's comings and goings are illuminated by charming copper lanterns and protected by the sheltering porch.

SITE LEGEND

1 Motor Court
2 Lawn Terrace
3 Outdoor Kitchen
4 Outdoor Dining
5 Pool Terrace
6 Sports Terrace

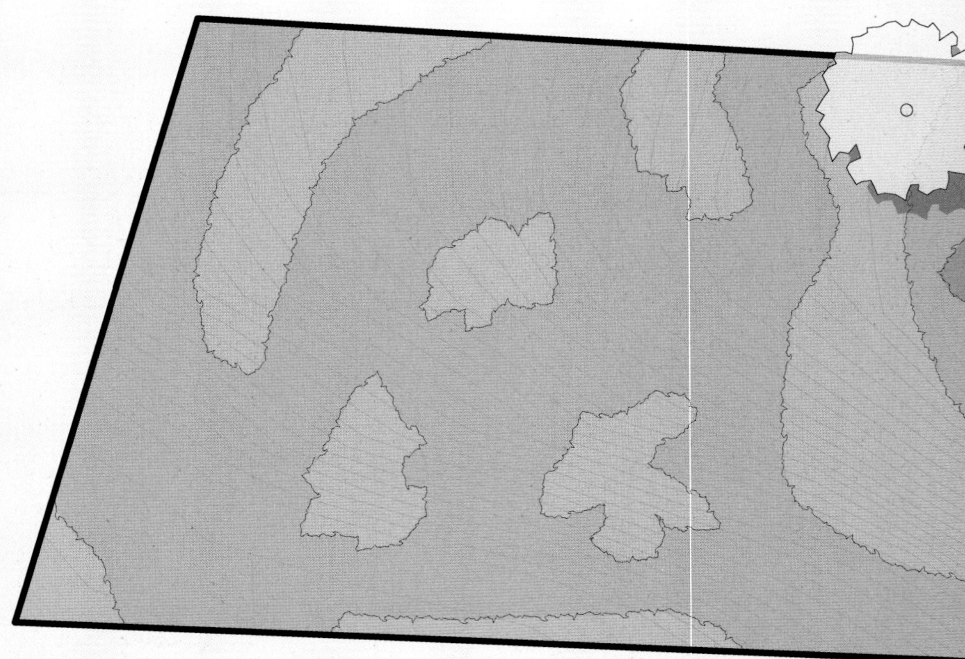

SITE PLAN

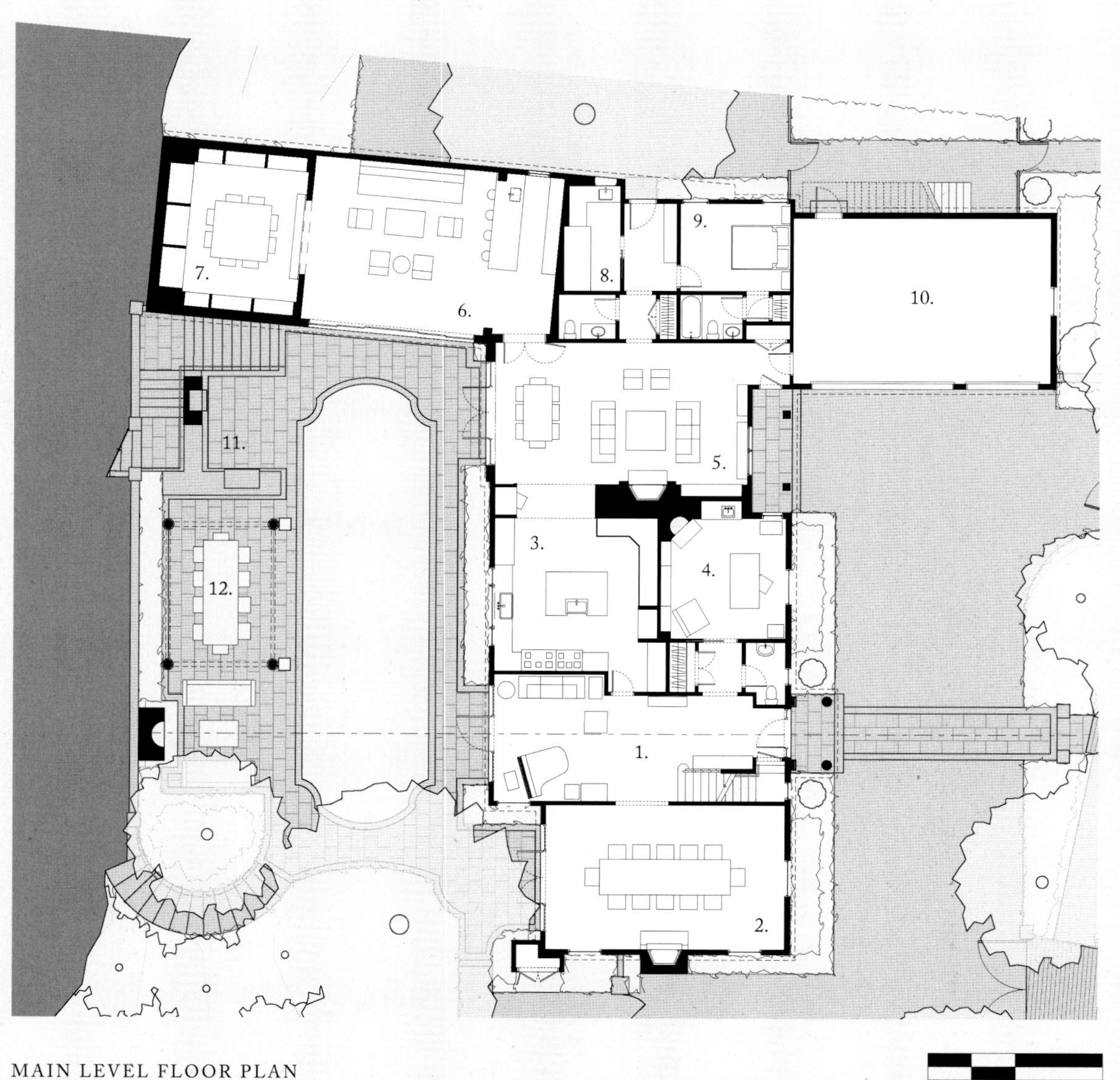

MAIN LEVEL FLOOR PLAN

PLAN LEGEND

1 Foyer
2 Dining Room
3 Kitchen
4 Office
5 Family Room
6 Sitting Room
7 Wine Room
8 Laundry
9 Guest Bedroom
10 Garage
11 Outdoor Kitchen
12 Outdoor Dining
13 Lounge
14 Primary Bedroom
15 Primary Bathroom
16 Gym
17 Children's Study
18 Bedroom
19 Pool
20 Pool House
21 Pergola

SECOND LEVEL FLOOR PLAN

DESERT HOUSE

Las Vegas, Nevada

When it comes to Mediterranean-style houses, I've always believed that outside of the actual Mediterranean region, the coastal climate of Southern California suits the style best. The ocean breeze, the complete indoor-outdoor lifestyle that welcomes loggias and embraces courtyards, and the year-round sun that makes exteriors more radiant, all helped shape my view. This world made sense. Until one day, when this idea was decidedly challenged.

On a seemingly ordinary morning, a potential client reached out asking me to design a Mediterranean-style home for her and her family. Nothing out of the ordinary there; fielding requests like this is typical for us. She then revealed its location: the Nevada desert. It was there, outside of Las Vegas, that a new house took form, and with it an entirely new paradigm.

OPPOSITE
Our inspiration to paint the bricks white came from the great architect Wallace Neff and his Libby Ranch in Ojai, California. As you walk through a portal in the tall hedge, a series of layers moves you from a public space to the very private inner sanctuary of the home.

Manifesting the Mediterranean idea in a desert environment, I discovered, works quite beautifully, and for the same reasons it works in coastal climates:

1. Courtyards, planted with trees and lush vegetation, provide shady places to take advantage of the outdoors.
2. Gracious loggias offer protected outdoor living space, here with a view of the lights of downtown Las Vegas. Though a departure from my usual views of nature, it still engages.
3. Thick walls provide insulation, and the recessed doors in those thick walls keep the sun at bay.
4. Covered spaces cast deep shadows even at the height of the day.
5. Pools and fountains offer more than just a way to cool off and nurture us physically. Water nurtures us psychologically as well, and helps set our minds at ease in the intense heat.

Creating multiple oases was one important consideration that drove the architectural design. Another major factor: how to make the best use of an oddly shaped parcel.

At the street, the lot is extremely narrow, broadening outward as it unfolds to the east. The shape presented us with a geometric challenge, as well as a great opportunity to use the

architecture to provide unexpected moments inside and out. We designed the house's geometry perpendicular to the view, and set out to create a serrated architectural profile. Each time the architecture reaches out and touches the landscape, and then darts back in, we found our opportunity to design an unexpected moment. And when the architecture pokes back out a little farther on, touches the landscape again, and then retreats, we designed another moment. This little dance of surprises goes on throughout the north side of the property and results in the house's variety of courtyards and garden spaces, each with its own personality and reason for being (beyond providing shade). One is related to the little breakfast room, another is passage-like, the third is more of a secret sitting area, and the last a spa courtyard. Often, they feature fountains whose sounds of trickling water help to calm, soothe, and somehow, almost magically, make the heat more tolerable.

The house's interior provided more opportunities to fine tune the Mediterranean vernacular for the desert environment. It also was a much appreciated chance to collaborate with an interior designer whose work I admire, Taylor Borsari. We had worked with her on projects before, but here, in addition to being the designer, she was also the client, adding a remarkable new level of personalization to our collaboration. Taylor's vision to simplify and lighten the architectural language aligned with my desire to push the style in new directions.

Working with a great interior designer makes our work even better and more unique. We looked forward to our weekly meetings, when we sought to discover the language of the house together. Room by room, we explored different ideas for details, and during the week, Taylor would further our explorations in plaster, wood, and tile. The hallmarks of Mediterranean design are all here, but are done in pared-back elegance. Ceilings are all whitewashed, but you can still see the wood's grain and roughness. Decorative details are there too, but are deliberately restrained and reserved for special moments. The thick and humble plank flooring is lightened, the plaster wall surfaces are plain, except for certain places like the front door and the bottom of the stairway where a lovely flourish gives it a moment to shine. The tilework on the stair risers, which, in the Spanish Mediterranean language, is usually colorful, here is monochromatic with a geometric pattern, and in the bathrooms, the tilework is subdued and geometric. Taylor's sparing use of details gives our eyes a chance to rest and appreciate each one before moving on to the next.

In a project that held so much design and collaborative joy, a favorite moment came with the design of the pool house, which I jokingly referred to as a "Temple to Aquatics." With three bays and plaster columns, the building is compact, and its planning is focused. Undiluted by complicated constraints, the structure gave us the chance to create a small and simple bit of classical symmetry.

RIGHT The two-story entry foyer carries the white brick of the outside to the inside. Throughout the house, we used hand-troweled plaster walls that require no paint; the color is integral to the plaster.

Remodelista
ROOM WITH A VIEW
commune
A ROOM of ONE'S OWN

We moved in a new direction with this house, often through Taylor's good-natured prodding, and I'm grateful for it. I enjoyed challenging my prior notion that the Mediterranean style only worked well along the 34th latitude, where Southern California sits in good company with southern Italy, southern Spain, and other coastal locales. This house proves that a contemporary lifestyle in a desert environment can be achieved through a modern Mediterranean approach. I was happy to have my paradigm shifted, and I'm happy at the thought of returning to the desert (covered in sunblock and under a wide-brimmed hat) to further refine my thoughts.

LEFT A traditional 1920s Spanish Colonial house would have dark beams, but we decided to whitewash them. It brightened the house while still retaining details of that style, like the scrolled brackets supporting the beams.

FOLLOWING Once again, Wallace Neff's architecture was inspirational, here seen in the fireplace, which merges into the wide windowsills to the left and right. The room's furnishings, not what you'd expect in a vintage Spanish Colonial house, offer a fresh point of view and counterpoint to the architecture in which they sit.

PATTERNS

In the Garden
FROM THE LAND
SURFING

LEFT
The monochromatic palette brings a sense of calm to the kitchen; it also lets the modern wicker lighting pendants become the focus, and true stars, of the room.

LEFT
I imagined this breakfast room as a sunny solarium. Its light comes from the peaceful courtyard just outside the windows.

OPPOSITE
The forms of the light fixtures are stunning on their own . . . and then comes the filigreed shadow patterns they cast onto the plaster walls, turning a simple hallway into an extraordinary experience.

FOLLOWING
Interior designer Taylor Borsari's abstracted, elegant white interiors are comfortable, cozy, and fanciful. Her restrained palette allows colorful pieces to really stand out, as with the sage-green bench at the foot of the bed.

etcetera
Gardenista

HICKENS
PATTERN
SEUNG-TAEK LEE

PREVIOUS
LEFT & RIGHT
His-and-hers sinks on the left and the makeup vanity on the right are treated similarly, with overscaled, curvaceous moldings defining the tops of their niches. These recessed areas, which feel deeply carved into the architecture, spring from a tradition in Spanish Colonial architecture.

OPPOSITE
Here in the desert, the loggia is so important, a shady spot to let the family enjoy the fresh air, even in the hot months. We referenced classical columns but made them simpler and more abstract so there was less to detract from the lush garden view.

RIGHT
We envisioned this space as sculpture, but also expanded the fireplace to include a niche for art and a bench for seating. The scrolled bracket is the same detail used in the living room's beam work.

LEFT
As the entire wall of glass pockets away to the left and disappears, the architecture is allowed to connect fully, and fluidly, to the landscape just beyond.

FOLLOWING LEFT
Fine-scale details in the ironwork and fountains of the garden spaces not only provide texture and interest; their decoration acts as a reminder of the world around us.

FOLLOWING RIGHT
Having the axis of the pool culminate in the siting of the pool house lends visual importance to the structure, highlighting a small but special place within the landscape.

PAGES 230–31
The house is a wonderful example of how you can take the language of the traditional Spanish Colonial style, update it for the way we live today, and do it all in a desert setting.

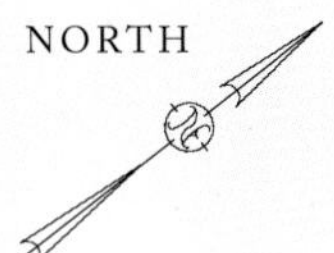

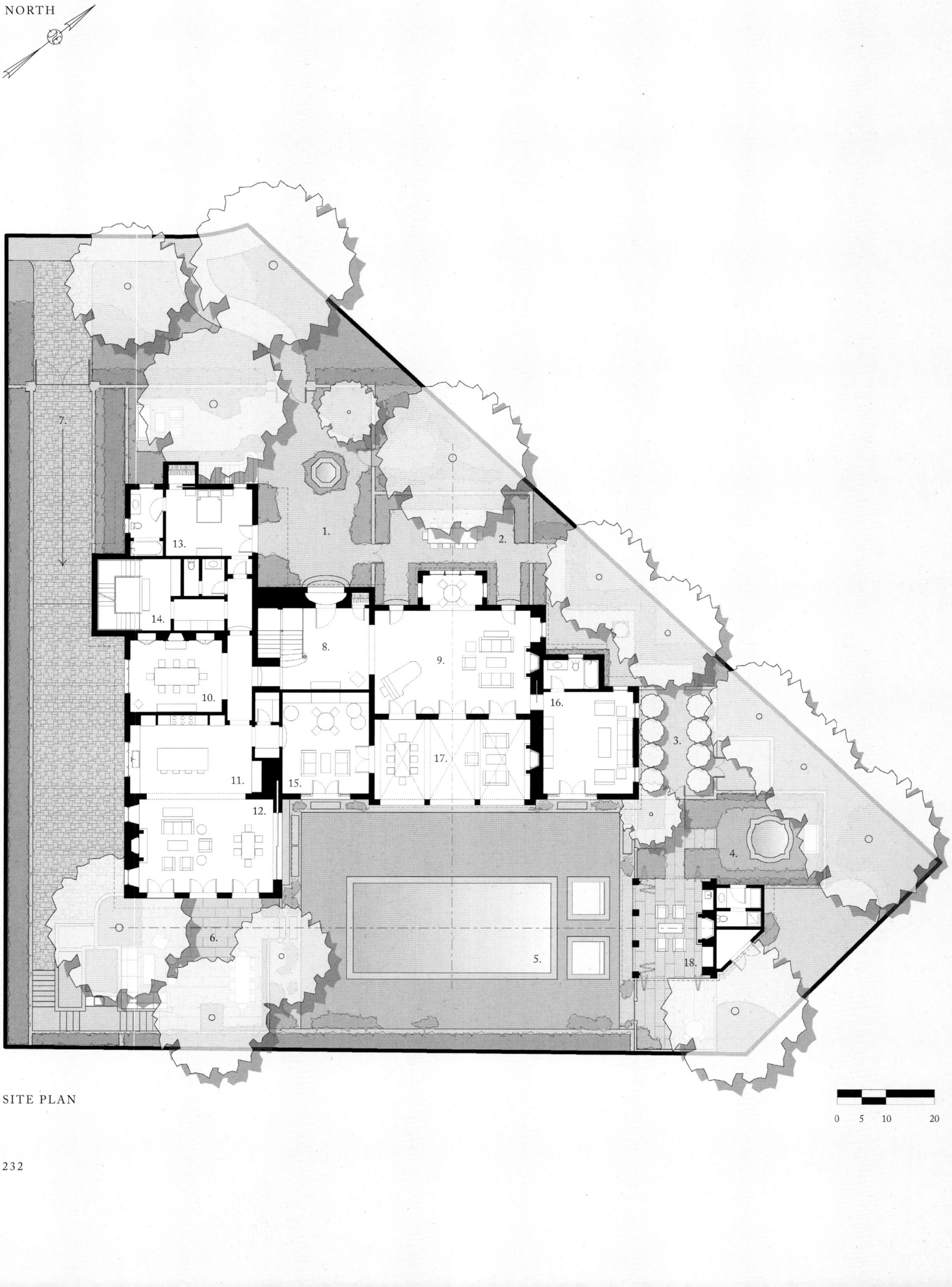

SITE PLAN

0 5 10 20

LEGEND

1 Entry Courtyard
2 Dining Courtyard
3 Fruit Tree Allée
4 Spa Garden
5 Pool
6 Entertainment Terrace
7 Ramp Down to Subterranean Garage
8 Foyer
9 Living Room
10 Dining Room
11 Kitchen
12 Family Room
13 Guest Bedroom
14 Back Stair Hall
15 Play Room
16 Theater
17 Loggia
18 Pool House
19 Upper Foyer
20 Primary Bedroom
21 Primary Closet
22 Primary Bathroom
23 Bedroom
24 Studio Office

MAIN LEVEL FLOOR PLAN

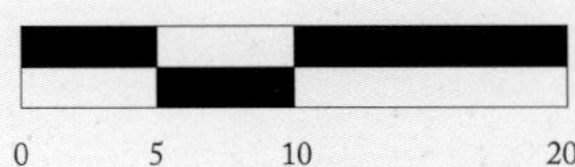

APPENDIX

DUME DRIVE

Architect: Evens Architects
Landscape Architect: Evens Architects
Interior Designer: Alana Homesley Interior Design
General Contractor: California Buildings, Inc.
Photographers: Karyn Millet and Erhard Pfeiffer

OLD AGOURA

Architect: Evens Architects
Landscape Architect: Evens Architects
Interior Designer: Joe Lucas
General Contractor: Jay Bruder, Bruder Construction
Photographer: Karyn Millet

PARRA GRANDE

Architect: Evens Architects
Landscape Architect: Evens Architects
Interior Designer: M. Elle Design
General Contractor: Kitchell Custom Homes
Photographer: Karyn Millet

STONE CANYON

Architect: Evens Architects
Landscape Architect: Evens Architects
Interior Designer: Windsor Smith Home
General Contractor: Aragon Fine Homes
Photographer: Karyn Millet

DESERT HOUSE

Design Architect: Evens Architects
Executive Architect: Richard Luke Architects
Landscape Architect: Evens Architects
Interior Designer: Taylor Borsari, Inc.
General Contractor: R. W. Bugbee & Associates
Photographer: Karyn Millet

PHOTOGRAPHY CREDITS

BLACKSTONE EDGE STUDIOS

Pages 40–41, 43

GREY CRAWFORD

Pages 45, 68, 95

ERIK EVENS

Pages 8, 9, 48

MANOLO LANGIS

Front cover; pages 1, 2, 11, 14–15, 16–17, 18–19, 20–21, 24, 26–27, 30–31, 32–33, 34, 35, 50, 56, 64–65, 66–67, 74–75, 76–77, 94 bottom right, 96–97, 98–99

KARYN MILLET

Pages 4, 7, 12, 22, 23, 28–29, 36–37, 38–39, 46, 51, 52–53, 54–55, 60, 61, 62–63, 70, 71, 72, 73, 78, 79, 80, 82, 83, 84–85, 86, 87, 88–89, 91, 92, 94 top left, 94 top right, 94 bottom left, 100–01, 103, 104, 108, 109, 110–11, 112–13, 114–15, 116–17, 120, 121, 129, 130–31, 132–33, 134–35, 136–37, 138–39, 140–41, 142, 143, 144–45, 146–47, 148, 149, 150–51, 152–153, 157, 158–59, 160–61, 162–63, 164–65, 166–67, 168–69, 170–71, 172–73, 174–75, 176–77, 178–79, 183, 184–85, 187, 188–89, 190–91, 192–93, 194–95, 196–97, 198–99, 200–01, 202–03, 204, 205, 209, 210–11, 212–13, 214–15, 216–17, 218, 219, 220–21, 222–23, 224, 225, 226–27, 228, 229, 230–31, 235, 236, 239

ERHARD PFEIFFER

Pages 42, 44, 49, 58–59, 90, 93, 106–07, 118–19, 122–23, 124–25

ACKNOWLEDGMENTS

I've always thought that designing and building homes feels like a miracle. We are tasked with creating an enormously complex and detailed object, made of disparate parts, never before built, with the goal of elevating our clients' lives. Though the journey is daunting, arrival at the destination is enormously gratifying and accomplished only with the talent, focus, and dedication of a host of collaborators. Writing this book was a similar journey. I am truly grateful to all the thoughtful people whose contributions led to our arrival at this destination.

Over the years, I have been blessed to work with extraordinary clients. Each in their own way, they have come to me with a broad vision and high expectations, and have trusted me to guide them in telling their story through architecture. My gratitude extends to all of them.

I am grateful to the gifted interior designers with whom I have collaborated, and it is truly a collaboration. I believe that a visionary interior designer brings their own unique point of view, one that takes the finished project to a higher level. Many thanks to all of the designers we have worked with, notably Chris Barrett, Michael Berman, Taylor Borsari, Marie Carson, Tim Clarke, Alana Homesley, Joe Lucas, and Windsor Smith.

To all the talented consultants, from structural engineers to lighting designers, I extend heartfelt thanks. Although my work begins as drawings on paper, the finished product is only as good as the final execution. I have been fortunate to work with so many skillful and ingenious contractors and craftspeople who have helped to turn my vision into buildable reality.

This book would not have been possible without the trust and support of my friends at Rizzoli. Thank you to Charles Miers and Ellen Cohen for believing in this project and helping me share my work. And special thanks to Sarah Gifford for her beautiful graphic design of this book.

The debt of thanks I owe to my principal photographer Karyn Millet is immense. Her keen eye and sharp talent have captured the essence of our work and made us look so good.

I want to extend my gratitude to Nancy Greystone, with whom I have spent many hours talking about my work and the philosophy behind it. Thank you for taking these ideas and helping me turn them into a story to share with the world.

My incredible team in the Evens Architects studio at KAA Design is truly the soul of our enterprise. Their talent, dedication, and passion for the work is what drives our firm, and their contributions have made the projects in this book possible. My heartfelt thanks to all of our team, past and present. And a special thanks to the people who have been right beside me leading our studio over the years: Sara Pijuan, David Vazquez, Michael McGowan, and John Margolis.

To Joyce Lopez, my guardian angel, thank you for supporting me every day, and keeping me on track as this process has unfolded. I truly could not have done it without you.

To my partners at KAA, Grant Kirkpatrick and Duan Tran, thank you for believing in my vision and my work, and for your brilliant leadership of our company. You inspire me daily.

To Keith Granet, who has always been there when I have needed him, thank you.

To Marc Appleton, who helped me see architecture in a different way, thank you for your mentorship, your friendship, and for writing the foreword to this book.

And finally, thank you, always and forever, to my children Teegan, Thomas, and Lauren. And to my wife, Robin, thank you for being with me on every moment of this journey. You have always been my rock. I love you all dearly.

Catalogue of the Dutch School
Catalogue of the Dutch School
HENRY MOORE ON SCULPTURE
WHISTLER
ART OF ANCIENT EGYPT
E.B.White
LINDBERGH
Thomas Wolfe
Les Misérables
HUGO
JACK LONDON
The Federalist
The Family MARK TWAIN
AYN RAND
ATLAS SHRUGGED
Shakespeare
ABRAHAM LINCOLN
ABRAHAM LINCOLN
astria

First published in the United States of America in 2024 by
Rizzoli International Publications, Inc.
300 Park Avenue South
New York, NY 10010
www.rizzoliusa.com

Text by ERIK EVENS with NANCY GREYSTONE
Foreword MARC APPLETON

Publisher CHARLES MIERS
Editor ELLEN R. COHEN
Production Manager KAIJA MARKOE
Managing Editor LYNN SCRABIS

Design SARAH GIFFORD

2024 2025 2026 2027 2028 / 10 9 8 7 6 5 4 3 2 1

ISBN: 978-0-8478-3445-7
Library of Congress Control Number: 2024934474

Printed in China